CRIMINAL LAW

Visit the *Law Express Series* Companion Website at
www.pearsoned.co.uk/lawexpress to find valuable **student**
learning material including:

▮ A Study Plan test to assess how well you know the subject
  before you begin your revision
▮ Interactive quizzes to test your knowledge of the main points
  from each chapter of the book
▮ Diagram plans for the questions in each chapter of the book
▮ Further examination questions and guidelines for answering
  them
▮ Interactive flashcards to help you revise the main cases
▮ Printable versions of the topic maps and checklists

LawExpress

Understand quickly. Revise effectively.
Take exams with confidence.

CRIMINAL LAW

ISBN: 1405823577

ENGLISH LEGAL SYSTEM

ISBN: 1405823585

EQUITY AND TRUSTS

ISBN: 1405821922

CONTRACT LAW

ISBN: 1405821957

TORT LAW

ISBN: 1405821949

LAND LAW

ISBN: 1405840218

CONSTITUTIONAL AND ADMINISTRATIVE LAW

ISBN: 1405821914

EU LAW

ISBN: 1405821930

Available from your local bookshop, or order online at
www.pearsoned.co.uk

Law Express

CRIMINAL LAW

Emily Finch

Stefan Fafinski

PEARSON

Longman

Harlow, England • London • New York • Boston • San Francisco • Toronto • Sydney • Singapore • Hong Kong
Tokyo • Seoul • Taipei • New Delhi • Cape Town • Madrid • Mexico City • Amsterdam • Munich • Paris • Milan

Pearson Education Limited

Edinburgh Gate

Harlow

Essex CM20 2JE

England

and Associated Companies throughout the world

Visit us on the World Wide Web at:
www.pearsoned.co.uk

First published 2007

ISBN–13: 978-1-4058-2357-9
ISBN–10: 1-4058-2357-7

British Library Cataloguing-in-Publication Data
A catalogue record for this book is available from the British Library

Library of Congress Cataloging-in-Publication Data
Fafinski, Stefan
    Criminal law / Stefan Fafinski, Emily Finch.
      p. cm.
    Includes bibliographical references and index.
    ISBN 1-4058-2357-7 (alk. paper)
     1. Criminal law--England. 2. Criminal law--Wales. I. Finch, Emily. II. Title.

  KD7869.F34 2007
  345.42--dc22

2006042857

10 9 8 7 6 5 4 3 2 1
11 10 09 08 07

Typeset by 3 in 10pt Helvetica Condensed
Printed and bound in China
EPC/01

The publisher's policy is to use paper manufactured from sustainable forests.

Contents

CONTENTS

Supporting resources

Visit **www.pearsoned.co.uk/lawexpress** to find valuable online resources

Companion Website for students

- A Study Plan test to assess how well you know the subject before you begin your revision
- Interactive quizzes to test your knowledge of the main points from each chapter of the book
- Diagram plans for the questions in each chapter of the book
- Further examination questions and guidelines for answering them
- Interactive flashcards to help you revise the main cases
- Printable versions of the topic maps and checklists

Also: The Companion Website provides the following features:

- Search tool to help locate specific items of content
- E-mail results and profile tools to send results of quizzes to instructors
- Online help and support to assist with website usage and troubleshooting

For more information please contact your local Pearson Education sales representative or visit **www.pearsoned.co.uk/lawexpress**

Acknowledgements

The authors would like to thank everyone – academics and students alike – who have contributed towards the many reviews of drafts of this book for their comments; even where a good point has meant some major reworking. In particular, we would like to thank Rebekah Taylor at Pearson Education for guiding us through the project and her endless patience during the process. Most importantly, we would like to thank everyone at the Island Farm Donkey Sanctuary in Oxfordshire for providing us with a peaceful place to which to run away when necessary, and Fernley Harris of The Byres, Galmpton, near Hope Cove in Devon where many of the earlier drafts of this book were written.

Emily Finch
Stefan Fafinski
March 2006

Publisher's acknowledgements

The publisher and authors would like to thank, in particular, the student reviewers Usman Mahmood, Tony Jennings and Michelle Lythgoe. Thanks also to the reviewers who contributed to the development of this series, including those students who participated in the research and focus groups, and helped to shape the series format.

Introduction

Criminal law is one of the core subjects required for a qualifying law degree so is a compulsory component on most undergraduate law programmes. Aspects of criminal law also appear in other subjects such as environmental law, family law and company law, as well as relating more directly to the study of criminal justice, evidence and criminology. As such, a thorough understanding of criminal law is vital for law students.

Crime is an integral part of everyday life. It is a prominent feature in the news and is a popular subject for fictional portrayal. Most students commencing legal studies will have some experience of crime whether this is direct, as a victim of crime, or indirectly through exposure to media coverage. This means that most offences covered on the syllabus such as murder, theft and rape will be familiar terms. This tends to give students the impression that they know more about criminal law than they do about other subjects on the syllabus. This can be a real disadvantage in terms of the academic study of criminal law because it tends to lead students to rely on preconceived notions of the nature and scope of the offences and to reach instinctive, but often legally-inaccurate, conclusions. It is absolutely essential to success in criminal law that you put aside any prior knowledge of the offences and focus on the principles of law derived from statutes and cases. By doing this, you will soon appreciate just how much difference there is between everyday conceptions of crime and its actuality.

This revision guide will help you to identify and apply the law and it provides frequent reminders of the importance of abandoning preconceptions about the offences. It is written to be used as a supplement to your course materials, lectures and textbooks. As a revision guide, it should do just that – guide you through revision; it should not be used to cut down on the amount of reading (or thinking) that you have to do in order to succeed. Criminal law is a vast and complex subject – you should realise this from looking at the size of your recommended textbook (which, incidentally, covers only a fraction of the criminal law that exists 'out there'). It follows that this revision guide could never be expected to cover the subject in the depth and detail required to succeed in exams and it does not set out to do so. Instead, it aims to provide a concise overall picture of the key areas for revision – reminding you of the headline points to enable you to focus your revision and identify the key points that you need to know.

REVISION NOTES

- Do not be misled by the familiarity of the offences; learn each topic afresh and focus on the legal meanings of the words that you encounter.

- Do rely on this book to guide you through the revision process.

- Do not rely on this book to tell you everything you need to know about criminal law.

- Make sure you consult your own syllabus frequently to check which topics are covered and in how much detail.

- Make use of your lecture notes, handouts, textbooks and other materials as you revise as these will ensure that you have sufficient depth of knowledge.

- Take every possible opportunity to practise your essay-writing and problem-solving technique; get as much feedback as you can.

- Be aware that many questions in criminal law combine different topics. Selective revision could leave you unable to answer questions which include reference to material that you have excluded from your revision.

Guided tour

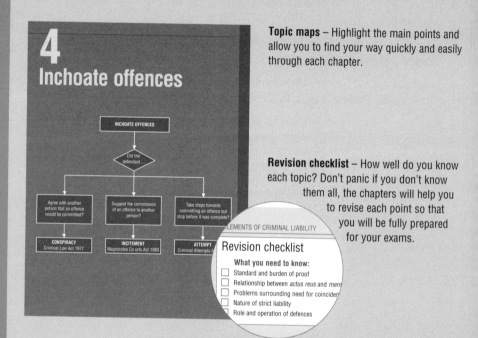

Topic maps – Highlight the main points and allow you to find your way quickly and easily through each chapter.

Revision checklist – How well do you know each topic? Don't panic if you don't know them all, the chapters will help you to revise each point so that you will be fully prepared for your exams.

Revision checklist

What you need to know:
- [ ] Standard and burden of proof
- [ ] Relationship between *actus reus* and *mens* [...]
- [ ] Problems surrounding need for coincide[...]
- [ ] Nature of strict liability
- [ ] Role and operation of defences

Sample questions – Prepare for what you will be faced with in your exams! Guidance on structuring strong answers is provided at the end of the chapter.

Sample question

Could you answer this question? Below is a typical problem question that could arise on this topic. Guidelines on answering the question are included at the end of the chapter, whilst a sample essay question and guidance on tackling it can be found on the companion website.

Key definition boxes – Make sure you understand essential legal terms.

KEY DEFINITIONS

Result crimes are those in which the *actus reus* is defined in terms of prohibited consequences irrespective of how these are brought about, i.e. causing death (murder). This differs from conduct crimes.

Conduct crimes are those in which the *actus reus* is concerned with prohibited behaviour regardless of its consequences.

Problem area boxes – Highlight areas where students most often trip up in exams. Use them to make sure you do not make the same mistakes.

of enforcing particular standa...
...harm.

Problem area:

A debate surrounds whether strict liability offenc...
in favour of their existence include:

■ *Promotion of care*: enforce regulations to prote...
■ *Deterrent value*: ensures compliance to avoid ...
■ *Easier enforcement*: no need to establish *men*...
corporations.
No risk to liberty: as offences are generally...
...ines rather than imprisonment.

...strong arguments exist that i...
...to impose liability wit...

KEY CASE

R v. *Steer* [1987] 2 All ER 833

Concerning: endangerment of life

Facts
As a result of a grudge against his former business partner, the defendant fired a rifle at the windows of his house, causing damage. Nobody inside the house was injured. The defendant's conviction for criminal damage with intent to endanger life was quashed by the House of Lords.

Legal principle
It must be the damage to property that endangers life not the means by which the property is damaged. Therefore, the defendant must have intended to endanger life by smashing windows or foreseen a risk that life would be endangered by smashing windows. The means by which the windows were smashed – firing a rifle – and the life-endangering potential of this method of damaging property were irrelevant and could not be used as a basis for liability.

Key case and key statutory provision boxes – Identify the essential cases and statutes that you need to know for your exams.

KEY STATUTORY PROVISION

Criminal Attempts Act 1981, s.1(1)

If, with intent to commit an offence to which this section applies, a person does an act which is more than merely preparatory to the commission of the offence, he is guilty of attempting to commit the offence.

Further thinking boxes – Illustrate areas of academic debate, and point you towards that extra reading required for the top grades.

FURTHER THINKING

An essay on oblique intention must demonstrate understanding of the progression of the case law. These articles provide clear outlines of the cases and the underlying policy issues in detail that is beyond the scope of this revision guide:

■ Norrie, A., 'After *Woollin*' [1999] *Criminal Law Review* 532
■ Simister, A.P. and Chan, W., 'Intention Thus Far' [1997] *Criminal Law Review* 740

Glossary – Forgotten the meaning of a word? – Where a word is highlighted in the text, turn to the glossary at the back of the book to remind yourself of its meaning.

Glossary of terms

Key definitions

Abetting	Implies consensus not causation
Aiding	Actual assistance, but neither consensus nor causation
Automatism	An act done by the muscles without any control by the mind
Battery	Any act by which a person intentionally or recklessly inflicts unlawful personal violence on another
Chain of causation	The link between the initial act of the defendant and the prohibited consequence
Common assault	An act by which a person intentionally or recklessly causes another to apprehend immediate and unlawful personal violence

Exam tips – Want to impress examiners? These indicate how you can improve your exam performance and your chances of getting top marks.

EXAM TIP

Failing to state the *mens rea* of the particular offence is a common mistake. Intention is a category of *mens rea*; it is *not* the *mens rea* of any offence. Many offences include intention within their *mens rea* but always in relation to the *actus reus*.

WRONG: The *mens rea* of murder is intention.
CORRECT: The *mens rea* of murder is intention to kill or cause GBH.

Always be sure that you can state the full and correct *mens rea* of each offence.

Revision notes – Highlight points that you should be aware of in other topic areas, or where your own course may adopt a specific approach that you should check with your course tutor before reading further.

REVISION NOTE

In addition to these requirements, it is essential that the defendant's act (or, in certain circumstances, omission) caused the victim's death. Causation and omissions are covered in Chapter 2, which you may like to revisit to refresh your memory.

Table of cases and statutes

Cases

Statutes

1
Elements of criminal liability

AR and MR must coincide	**ACTUS REUS** (prohibited act)	or **STRICT LIABILITY** (*actus reus* only, no *mens rea* requirement)
	MENS REA (culpable state of mind)	

ABSENCE OF A VALID DEFENCE

CRIMINAL LIABILITY

Revision checklist

What you need to know:

☐ Standard and burden of proof
☐ Relationship between *actus reus* and *mens rea*
☐ Problems surrounding need for coincidence of *actus reus* and *mens rea*
☐ Nature of strict liability
☐ Role and operation of defences

Introduction:
Understanding Criminal Liability

Criminal liability is based upon a combination of actions (*actus reus*) and thoughts (*mens rea*).

This is expressed by the maxim *actus non facit reum nisi mens sit rea* which means that *an act alone will not give rise to criminal liability unless it was done with a guilty state of mind.*

If *actus reus* and *mens rea* are established and there is no valid defence, the defendant is guilty. The onus is on the prosecution (burden of proof) to establish the elements of the offence beyond reasonable doubt (standard of proof).

It is important not to overlook the foundations of criminal liability as part of the revision process as a grasp of this material provides an essential foundation upon which an understanding of the operation of the substantive offences is based. There is also potential for exam questions that tackle these basic issues.

Essay question advice

Essay questions on the relationship between *actus reus* and *mens rea* are common. They require the student to have a good grasp of basic principles and an ability to discuss the underlying rationale of the law. Questions on strict liability also arise frequently and should involve a discussion of how these offences depart from general criminal law principles which require a culpable state of mind.

Problem question advice

Coincidence of *actus reus* and *mens rea* may form part of a problem question. Knowledge of the elements of criminal liability and their operation is essential even if it does not arise directly in a question as it would be impossible to answer any problem question without understanding how *actus reus*, *mens rea* and defences work in combination.

Sample question

Could you answer this question? Below is a typical essay question that could arise on this topic. Guidelines on answering the question are included at the end of the chapter, whilst a sample problem question and guidance on tackling it can be found on the companion website.

Essay question

How accurately is the maxim *actus non facit reum nisi mens sit rea* reflected in criminal law?

■ *Actus reus* and *mens rea*

These are the building blocks of criminal liability. In simple terms, *actus reus* (AR) is the guilty act and *mens rea* (MR) is the guilty mind, both of which are required for criminal liability.

The precise nature of the *actus reus* and *mens rea* are determined by the particular offence. For example, the *actus reus* of criminal damage is the damage/destruction of property belonging to another whilst the *mens rea* of murder is intention to kill or cause GBH (grevious bodily harm). The definition of the offence, in statute or common law, will contain the elements of the offence.

EXAM TIP

Failing to state the *mens rea* of the particular offence is a common mistake. Intention is a category of *mens rea*; it is *not* the *mens rea* of any offence. Many offences include intention within their *mens rea* but always in relation to the *actus reus*.

WRONG: The *mens rea* of murder is intention.
CORRECT: The *mens rea* of murder is intention to kill or cause GBH.

Always be sure that you can state the full and correct *mens rea* of each offence.

REVISION NOTE

More detailed examination of AR and MR can be found in the following chapters. In addition to this, make sure that you can state the AR and MR of each substantive offence; this is a valuable part of the revision process.

Coincidence of *actus reus* and *mens rea*

It is not enough that the defendant has committed the guilty act and then later formed the guilty state of mind (or *vice versa*): the two must coincide. This means that the defendant must possess the guilty state of mind *at the time* that the *actus reus* is committed (see Figure 1.1).

Problems arise in fixing liability if there is a lapse in time after the *actus reus* before the *mens rea* comes into being and, equally, in situations where the *mens rea* precedes the *actus reus*.

Actus reus occurring before *mens rea*

Two distinct approaches have been used to secure a conviction in situations where the *actus reus* is complete prior to the formation of *mens rea*:

- treating the *actus reus* as a *continuing act* (*Fagan*) (see page 6): and,
- basing liability on *failure to act* after creating a dangerous situation (*Miller*) (see page 7).

EXAM TIP

Lack of coincidence is a popular examination topic. You will need to be able to explain why lack of coincidence is a problem and how the courts have tackled this. A good grasp of cases such as *Fagan*, *Miller* and *Church* is important as the facts demonstrate the problems with lack of coincidence and the judgments illustrate the creativity of the judiciary in overcoming this impediment to conviction.

Figure 1.1

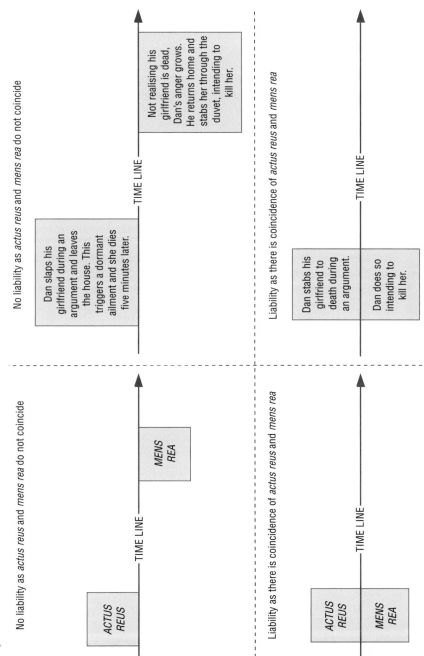

No liability as *actus reus* and *mens rea* do not coincide

Dan slaps his girlfriend during an argument and leaves the house. This triggers a dormant ailment and she dies five minutes later.

Not realising his girlfriend is dead, Dan's anger grows. He returns home and stabs her through the duvet, intending to kill her.

TIME LINE

No liability as *actus reus* and *mens rea* do not coincide

ACTUS REUS

MENS REA

TIME LINE

Liability as there is coincidence of *actus reus* and *mens rea*

Dan stabs his girlfriend to death during an argument.

Dan does so intending to kill her.

TIME LINE

Liability as there is coincidence of *actus reus* and *mens rea*

ACTUS REUS

MENS REA

TIME LINE

KEY CASE

Fagan v. *Metropolitan Police Commissioner* [1969] 1 QB 439

Concerning: coincidence of *actus reus* and *mens rea*

Facts

The defendant accidentally stopped his car on a policeman's foot but then refused to move when he realised this. He appealed against his conviction for assaulting a police officer in the execution of his duty on the basis that at the time of the *actus reus* (when his car made contact with the policeman's foot) he had no *mens rea* (because it was accidental) and by the time he formed *mens rea* (refusing to move) there was no act upon which to base liability (he merely refused to undo that which he had already done).

Legal principle

It was held that the *actus reus* of assault (in the sense of a battery) came into being when contact was first made between the car and the policeman's foot. This *actus reus* continued for the whole time that the car remained on the foot, only ending when the car was moved. At the point in time that the defendant became aware of the contact and refused to move, he developed the requisite *mens rea* and liability was complete.

EXAM TIP

It can be useful to scribble down a timeline of events to clarify when the *actus reus* and *mens rea* occurred as Figure 1.2 demonstrates in relation to *Fagan*. This is particularly useful when facing a problem question on coincidence as it can be difficult otherwise to determine 'what happened when' from the mass of facts included in the question.

The use of a continuing *actus reus* can only provide a solution if there is some ongoing conduct (the car remained on the foot). It cannot overcome lack of coincidence if the *actus reus* is complete (if the defendant had driven over the foot).

An alternative approach was formulated in *Miller* to deal with a situation in which the *actus reus* was complete prior to formation of *mens rea* (see Figure 1.3).

Figure 1.2

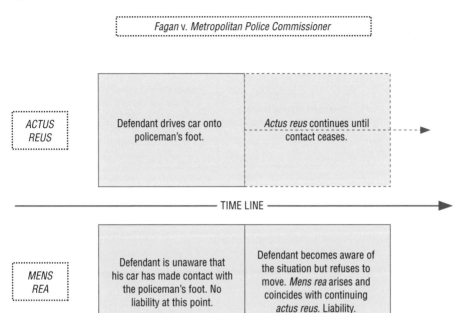

KEY CASE

R v. *Miller* [1983] 2 AC 161

Concerning: coincidence of *actus reus* and *mens rea*

Facts

The defendant fell asleep in a derelict house whilst smoking a cigarette. He awoke to find the mattress smouldering but merely moved to a different part of the house. The house was damaged in the ensuing fire. Here, the act causing the *actus reus* (dropping the cigarette) occurred when the defendant was asleep and the *mens rea* (recklessness as to the damage or destruction of property) arose when he awoke.

Legal principle

The House of Lords held that the defendant had created a dangerous situation which gave rise to a duty to act. Therefore, the *actus reus* was satisfied by the defendant's failure to deal with the fire and this coincided with the relevant *mens rea* thus he was liable.

Figure 1.3

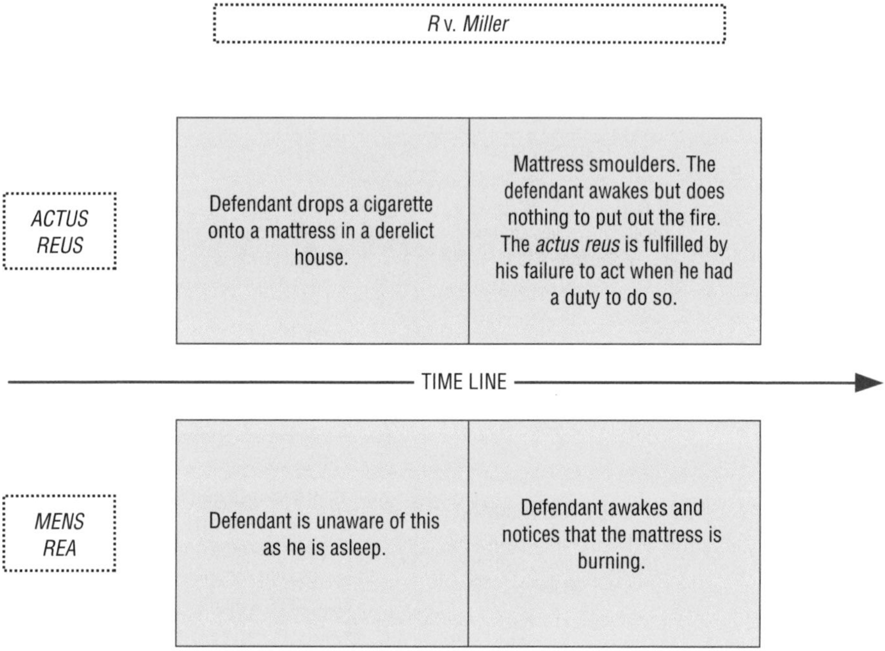

R v. *Miller*

ACTUS REUS	Defendant drops a cigarette onto a mattress in a derelict house.	Mattress smoulders. The defendant awakes but does nothing to put out the fire. The *actus reus* is fulfilled by his failure to act when he had a duty to do so.

──────────── TIME LINE ────────────▶

MENS REA	Defendant is unaware of this as he is asleep.	Defendant awakes and notices that the mattress is burning.

Mens rea occurring before *actus reus*

Neither of the solutions formulated in *Fagan* or *Miller* are able to deal with situations in which the *mens rea* occurs prior to the *actus reus* so further judicial creativity was necessary. This resulted in the *single transaction* view.

KEY CASE

R v. *Church* [1966] 1 QB 59

Concerning: coincidence of *actus reus* and *mens rea*

Facts

The defendant attacked a woman intending to cause her GBH (MR). She lapsed into unconsciousness but the defendant believed she was dead so he threw her body into a river in order to dispose of it. The victim subsequently drowned (AR).

Legal principle

A defendant will be liable if the entire incident viewed as a whole could be viewed as a 'series of events' designed to cause death or GBH. The elements of the offence will be satisfied provided the *actus reus* and *mens rea* occur somewhere during a single transaction.

A defendant cannot have an intention to kill a person if he believes that person is already dead. By viewing the events as a whole – a single transaction – the courts were able to impose liability but at the expense of strict legal principles that require the *actus reus* and *mens rea* to exist at one single point in time (see Figure 1.4).

Figure 1.4

	R v. Church	
ACTUS REUS	Defendant attacks victim. She does not die. No *actus reus* of murder.	Defendant throws unconscious woman into river to dispose of the body. As a result, the victim drowned thus fulfilling the *actus reus* of murder.

TIME LINE ⟶

MENS REA	Defendant intends to cause GBH thus satisfying the *mens rea* of murder.	Defendant did not intend to kill the victim at this point as he believed she was already dead. It was held that he was liable as the whole incident was a 'series of events' designed to cause death.

■ Strict liability

Strict liability offences do not require *mens rea* in relation to all parts of the *actus reus*. This means that a defendant can be convicted even if he was unaware of essential matters relevant to the offence. For example:

- A defendant can be convicted of driving whilst disqualified even if he believes his disqualification period has ended (*Bowsher* [1973] RTR 202).
- Liability can be imposed for selling a lottery ticket to a person under 16 even if the defendant did not realise the age of the customer (*Harrow LBC* v. *Shah* [2000] 1 WLR 83).

Strict liability offences are almost inevitably created by statute and are often regarded as 'regulatory offences' where there is no moral content to the offence, such as laws relating to trading standards and road traffic offences. Strict liability offences are seen as a way of enforcing particular standards of behaviour and thus protecting the public from harm.

Problem area:

A debate surrounds whether strict liability offences should exist at all. The arguments in favour of their existence include:

■ *Promotion of care*: enforce regulations to protect people from harm.
■ *Deterrent value*: ensures compliance to avoid criminal prosecution.
■ *Easier enforcement*: no need to establish *mens rea*, particularly useful in respect of corporations.
■ *No risk to liberty*: as offences are generally regulatory and lead to the imposition of fines rather than imprisonment.

However, strong arguments exist that it is contrary to fundamental principles of criminal law to impose liability without fault, i.e. in the absence of a culpable state of mind. The European Court of Human Rights suggests strict liability is not appropriate in offences conferring serious criminal liability (*Salabiaku* v. *France* (1988) 13 EHRR 379). Equally, the House of Lords has recently emphasised that there should be a presumption of *mens rea* (or a presumption against strict liability) in all statutory offences: *B* v. *DPP* [2000] 2 AC 428; *R* v. *K* [2001] 3 FCR 115.

An excellent outline of the opposing arguments that incorporate discussion of recent case law developments and an examination of the theoretical justification for strict liability can be found in Horder, J., 'Strict Liability, Statutory Construction and the Spirit of Liberty' (2002) 118 LQR 458–475.

EXAM TIP

It is unusual to encounter a problem question involving strict liability but essays are commonplace. Some will make it clear that a discussion of strict liability is required, such as 'Discuss the role of strict liability offences in modern criminal law'. Others, however, are less direct so be alert for references to 'fault' or 'mental states' as a clue that an essay involves strict liability: for example, 'There should be no criminal liability without fault. Discuss.' (Note that this question could involve other issues raised in this chapter, such as the coincidence of AR and MR.)

■ Defences

Strictly speaking, a defence is a means by which the defendant is able to avoid criminal liability even if the *actus reus* and *mens rea* have been established. However, some things which are often described as defences are actually *denials* of part of the offence. Defences fall into four categories (Figure 1.5):

Figure 1.5

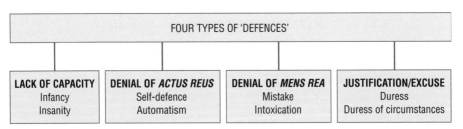

Defences may be:

■ general (available for any offence), e.g. insanity
■ particular (limited to specific offences), e.g. provocation is only a defence to murder
■ complete (results in an acquittal), e.g. automatism
■ partial (results in reduction of liability), e.g. diminished responsibility reduces murder to manslaughter

REVISION NOTE

Individual defences, their operation and effect are considered in more detail in later chapters.

EXAM TIP

An essay question on defences generally (as opposed to an essay about a particular defence) requires an understanding of the role that the different types of defence play in negating criminal liability. It should not contain a detailed description of the operation of specific defences but should use brief examples to demonstrate the operation of different types of defence.

Chapter summary:
Putting it all together

☐ Can you tick all the points from the revision checklist at the beginning of this chapter?

☐ Take the **end-of-chapter quiz** on the companion website.

☐ Test your knowledge of the cases with the **revision flashcards** on the website.

☐ Attempt the essay question from the beginning of the chapter using the guidelines below.

☐ Go to the companion website to try out other questions.

Answer guidelines

See the essay question at the start of the chapter. A diagram illustrating how to structure your answer is available on the website.

This is actually a straightforward question but it appears off-putting because it is not immediately clear what it requires. The key to answering questions like this is to unpick them and work out what they require. The Latin phrase means that there is no criminal liability for conduct unless it is accompanied by a guilty mind; in other words, no liability without *mens rea*. The ability to explain the meaning of the maxim and give some examples of the rule and exceptions to it should secure a solid mark for this question. An ability to demonstrate an understanding of the underlying theoretical issues and to engage in analysis of the merits of the current law will make your answer stand out and ensure greater success.

1 Explain the maxim. Use examples to demonstrate its operation, such as the need for both AR and MR as the basis for liability. Explain why the maxim is important with particular reference to concepts such as fault, blame and culpability.
2 Remember that there are marks available for doing simple things well. For example, do not forget to include an explanation of AR and MR.
3 Discussion of the attempts by the courts to overcome lack of coincidence of AR and MR demonstrate the importance of the maxim. Incorporate key cases noted above (remembering to use the facts sparingly and focus on the principle).
4 Identify exceptions to the general rule, for example, strict liability offences and explain the rationale for their existence.
5 Conclude by drawing together the strands of argument in a way that directly addresses the question. Given the number of exceptions you have identified, is the

maxim still important? Or, is its importance emphasised by the lengths that the courts will go to in order to find coincidence of AR and MR?

Make your answer really stand out

■ *Incorporate academic opinion.* Have you read an article that deals with the topic that you can mention in your answer? Can you summarise the views of leading academics on the topic?

■ *Use case law effectively.* Avoid the temptation to outline the facts in detail; remember, it is the legal principle that is important and the facts should only be included to the extent that they are necessary to explain the principle. Marks are lost for lengthy descriptive sections that do not develop the argument.

2
Actus reus

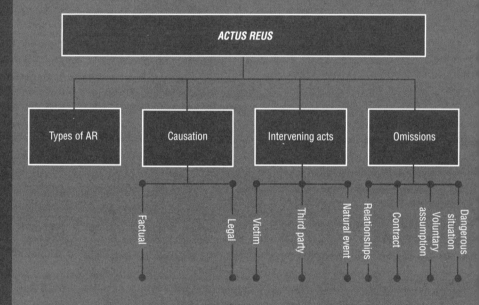

Revision checklist

What you need to know:

- [ ] Types of *actus reus*
- [ ] Role of *actus reus* in establishing criminal liability
- [ ] Relationship between factual and legal causation
- [ ] Circumstances when intervening acts will break the chain of causation
- [ ] Situations giving rise to liability for failing to act

Introduction:
Understanding *actus reus*

Actus reus is often described as the 'guilty act' or 'conduct element' of an offence but is more correctly described as *all the external elements of the offence*.

In other words, everything apart from the defendant's state of mind.

All offences have an *actus reus* so the issues covered in this chapter could arise in relation to any offence making this an important revision topic. Revising issues such as causation and omissions provides an excellent foundation for coursework or exam problem questions so make sure you have a firm grasp of these before revising the substantive offences.

Essay question advice

Essays involving *actus reus* fall into two categories.

1 Broad questions dealing with the nature of *actus reus* and its role in establishing criminal liability. These require *breadth* of knowledge and ability to select relevant examples in support of your argument.

2 Narrower questions focusing on particular issues such as the policy underlying causation or the rationale for imposing liability for omissions. These require greater *depth* of knowledge. Make sure you know *enough* about a topic before attempting to answer a question.

Problem question advice

Problem questions arise in conjunction with substantive offences, frequently homicide (causation) and criminal damage (omissions), so it is important to revise these topics thoroughly in conjunction with the material covered in this chapter.

Sample question

Could you answer this question? Below is a typical problem question that could arise on this topic. Guidelines on answering the question are included at the end of the chapter, whilst a sample essay question and guidance on tackling it can be found on the companion website.

Problem question

Darius attacks Veronica, leaving her unconscious. Adam and Bernard walk past. Adam does nothing but Bernard, experienced in first aid, attempts to treat Veronica but gives up after a few moments because he is late for a meeting. At the hospital, Dr Eric fails to spot Veronica's head injuries and assumes she is unconscious because she is drunk. Veronica dies from her injuries two hours later. The inquest determines that she would have survived had she received prompt treatment.

Discuss the criminal liability of the parties.

■Types of *actus reus*

The *actus reus* covers all external elements of an offence, going far beyond its common characterisation as a 'guilty act' (see Figure 2.1).

EXAM TIP

Understanding of the different types of *actus reus* should ensure that you are able to look for all the elements of the *actus reus* in the facts of a problem question, ensuring that no aspect of the offence is omitted from your answer.

Figure 2.1

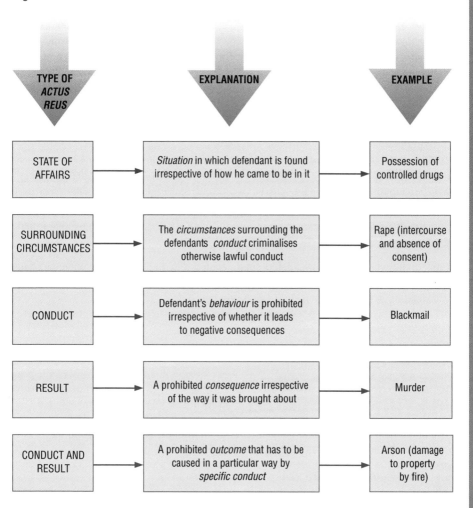

TYPE OF *ACTUS REUS*	EXPLANATION	EXAMPLE
STATE OF AFFAIRS	*Situation* in which defendant is found irrespective of how he came to be in it	Possession of controlled drugs
SURROUNDING CIRCUMSTANCES	The *circumstances* surrounding the defendants *conduct* criminalises otherwise lawful conduct	Rape (intercourse and absence of consent)
CONDUCT	Defendant's *behaviour* is prohibited irrespective of whether it leads to negative consequences	Blackmail
RESULT	A prohibited *consequence* irrespective of the way it was brought about	Murder
CONDUCT AND RESULT	A prohibited *outcome* that has to be caused in a particular way by *specific conduct*	Arson (damage to property by fire)

■ Causation

KEY DEFINITIONS

Result crimes are those in which the *actus reus* is defined in terms of prohibited consequences irrespective of how these are brought about, i.e. causing death (murder). This differs from conduct crimes.

Conduct crimes are those in which the *actus reus* is concerned with prohibited behaviour regardless of its consequences.

As result crimes are concerned with consequences, the nature of the act that brought the consequences about is unimportant, provided it caused the consequence. For example, there is no requirement that death is caused by unlawful means, just a requirement that death is caused. Therefore, the *actus reus* of murder is equally satisfied if the defendant shoots the victim (unlawful act) or gives him a piece of cake that induces an extreme allergic reaction (lawful act) provided that death results.

This is why *causation* plays such a central role in criminal law.

KEY DEFINITION

Chain of causation This provides a link between the initial act of the defendant (which need not be unlawful) and the prohibited consequence which has occurred. This is why it forms part of the *actus reus*: it is not enough that the prohibited consequence has occurred, it must be caused by the defendant.

This chapter will focus on causation in murder but the principles are applicable to all result crimes (see Figure 2.2).

A defendant will be liable for causing death, even if it is an indirect consequence of his act, provided the **chain of causation** between act and consequence is unbroken.

Causation is established using a two-stage test (Figure 2.3):

Factual causation

KEY DEFINITION

Factual causation The defendant's act must be a *sine qua non* of the prohibited consequence. This means that the consequence would not have occurred without the defendant's actions. Factual causation is established using the 'but for' test.

KEY CASE

R v. *White* [1910] 2 KB 124

Concerning: 'but for' test, factual causation

Facts

The defendant wanted to kill his mother. He poisoned her drink but she died of natural causes before the poison took effect.

Legal principle

Factual causation is established by asking whether the victim would have died '*but for*' the defendant's conduct. If the answer is 'yes', the defendant did not cause death. The defendant's mother would have died anyway thus he is not the factual cause of death.

Figure 2.2

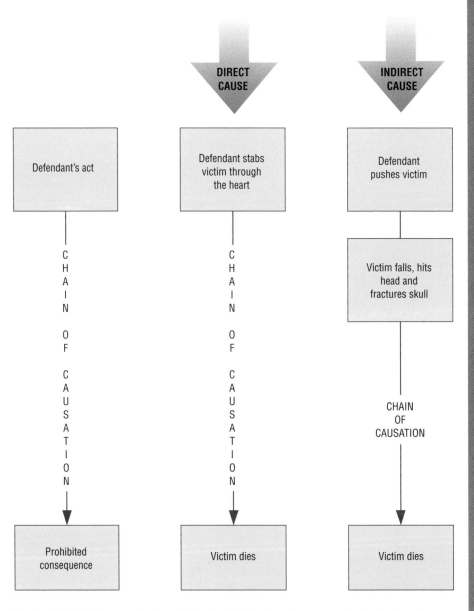

The 'but for' test is a preliminary filter that eliminates all unconnected acts/events leaving a range of potential legal causes. Consider the scenarios in Figure 2.4.

Figure 2.3

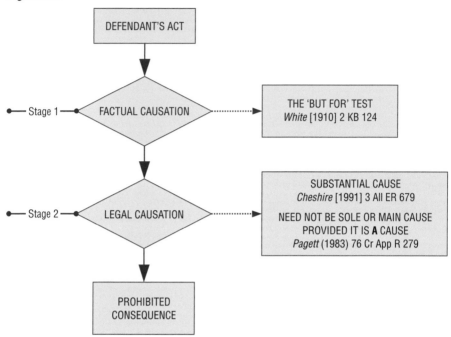

Figure 2.4

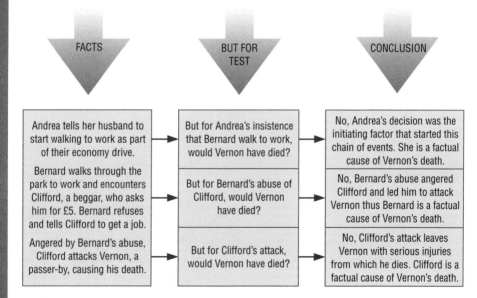

The 'but for' test establishes multiple factual causes of death. Not all factual causes make a meaningful contribution to death nor do factual causes imply blameworthiness. Factual causes merely establish a preliminary connection between act and consequence.

Legal causation

It would be unthinkable to base liability on factual causes alone as these are often too remote from the prohibited consequence. For example, Andrea should not be criminally liable for Vernon's death merely because she told Bernard to walk to work. Legal causation as a policy-driven notion uses notions of culpability, responsibility and foreseeability to select the most appropriate, i.e. blameworthy, factual cause as the basis for liability, even if this is not the most immediate cause of death.

KEY CASE

R v. *Pagett* (1983) 76 Cr App R 279

Concerning: legal causation, multiple causes

Facts

To avoid arrest, the defendant used his pregnant girlfriend as a shield and fired at armed police. The police returned fire, hitting and killing the girl. The defendant was held to be the legal cause of death despite causing no physical injury himself as he set in motion the chain of events that led to death and it was foreseeable that the police would return fire.

Legal principle

It was held that the defendant's act need not be the sole cause, or even the main cause, of death provided it is *a* cause in that it 'contributed significantly to that result' (*per* Robert Goff LJ at 290).

Pagett is a good illustration of the policy underlying legal causation. He did not fire the shot that killed the victim but he was liable for her death as his was the most *blameworthy* act in the events leading to her death. This approach is reflected in the medical negligence cases in which only 'palpably wrong' medical treatment will relieve the person inflicting the initial wound of liability (see Figure 2.5).

The defendant in *Cheshire* remained liable despite the contribution of the negligent treatment to the victim's death because the defendant's wrongdoing put the victim in the position where medical treatment was needed. As the House of Lords said in *Cheshire*, misdiagnosis and routine errors are inevitable and it is therefore foreseeable as a result of causing a person to suffer injury. Only in cases such as *Jordan* where

Figure 2.5

R v. *Jordan* (1956) 40 Cr App R 152
FACTS The defendant stabbed the victim who was taken to hospital. The wound healed but the victim died following an allergic reaction to drugs administered at the hospital.
DEFENDANTS CONTRIBUTION TO DEATH The initial stab wound.
OTHER CONTRIBUTION(S) TO DEATH The hospital's failure to note the victim's allergy and the administration of drugs that prompted an allergic reaction.
OUTCOME The defendant was not liable as the original wound had healed and the medical treatment was 'palpably wrong' thus breaking the link between the defendant's act and the victim's death.

R v. *Cheshire* [1991] 3 All ER 670
FACTS The defendant shot the victim in the leg and stomach, necessitating hospital treatment. The victim suffered complications following a tracheotomy which the hospital failed to recognise.
DEFENDANT'S CONTRIBUTION TO DEATH The initial gunshot wounds.
OTHER CONTRIBUTION(S) TO DEATH The poor standard of care following the tracheotomy which caused respiratory complications from which the victim died.
OUTCOME It was accepted that the original injuries were no longer life-threatening and that the victim would not have died had he received appropriate care following the tracheotomy. However, the need for the tracheotomy flowed from the defendant's original act thus he remained liable.

the treatment given to the victim was '*palpably wrong*' would it break the chain of causation and remove liability for causing death from the defendant.

Problem area: multiple causes of death

As *Pagett* and *Cheshire* demonstrate, the most immediate cause of death is not always the legal cause. To put it another way, supervening acts which contribute to death will not necessarily absolve the defendant of liability for causing death. Therefore, it is not always a straightforward matter to select which of the causes of death will be the legal cause.

Glanville Williams describes legal causation as a 'moral reaction' that determines 'whether the result can fairly be said to be imputable to the defendant'. In cases involving multiple causes, follow the chain of events backwards from death in search of the *most culpable act* as this will usually be the legal cause.

Intervening acts

KEY DEFINITION

Intervening act An intervening act (*novus actus interveniens*) is something which occurs *after* the defendant's act that breaks the chain of causation and relieves the defendant of responsibility for the prohibited consequence. As *Cheshire* demonstrates, not all events that occur after the defendant's act will break the chain of causation. Circumstances will only break the chain of causation if they are:

(a) an overwhelming cause of death; and
(b) an unforeseeable occurrence.

Intervening acts fall into three categories:

1 acts of the victim
2 acts of third parties
3 naturally occurring events.

Victim's actions

The general rule of causation is that the defendant is liable for the foreseeable consequences of his actions. Therefore, the victim may break the chain of causation if his reaction to the defendant's initial act is extreme and unforeseeable.

KEY CASE

R v. Roberts (1971) 56 Cr App R 95

Concerning: intervening acts, victim's reaction

Facts

The defendant interfered with the victim's clothing whilst she was a passenger in his car. She jumped from the moving vehicle and sustained serious injuries in the fall. The defendant denied causing these injuries but his conviction was upheld as it was foreseeable that the victim would attempt to escape and could be injured in doing so.

Legal principle

The chain of causation will be broken only if the victim's actions were 'so daft' as to be unforeseeable.

Roberts makes it clear that only extreme acts of the victim will break the chain of causation and relieve the defendant of liability. This must be considered in conjunction with the **'thin-skull' rule**.

KEY DEFINITION

Thin-skull rule This provides that a defendant is liable for the full extent of the victim's injuries even if, due to some abnormality or pre-existing condition, the victim suffers greater harm as a result of the defendant's actions than the 'ordinary' victim would suffer.

The thin-skull rule is an exception to the rule that the defendant is only liable for the foreseeable consequences of his actions.

The leading case is *Blaue* [1975] 1 WLR 1411. The defendant stabbed the victim, puncturing her lung. She refused a blood transfusion as it was contrary to her religious beliefs. The defendant was convicted of manslaughter even though the victim had refused treatment that would have saved her life. It was held that the thin-skull rule was not limited to physical conditions but included an individual's psychological make-up and beliefs.

FURTHER THINKING

The issue of whether the victim's self-administration of a drug breaks the chain of causation between the dealer's supply and the victim's death has been particularly challenging. There are excellent articles providing comprehensive analysis of the issues and succinct summaries of the relevant cases that would be valuable reading prior to writing an essay on this issue, for example:

■ Heaton, R., 'Dealing in Death' [2003] *Criminal Law Review* 497
■ Ormerod, D.C. and Fortson, R., 'Drug Dealers as Manslaughterers (Again)' [2005] *Criminal Law Review* 819.

Third parties

Third parties may intervene between the defendant's act and the victim's death in a number of ways. There may be a subsequent attack on the victim, for example, or an unsuccessful attempt to assist the victim that worsens his condition or causes fresh injuries.

In a problem question involving third-party intervention, consider (1) how significant their contribution was to death and (2) whether their actions were foreseeable.

For example, if the defendant inflicted minor burns upon the victim and the ambulance driver accidentally drove into a river causing the victim to die, it is arguable that this rendered the defendant's initial injury insignificant and was wholly unforeseeable thus breaking the chain of causation. Always remember the powerful counter-argument that the victim would not have needed the ambulance without the defendant's actions.

Naturally-occurring events

Again, principles of foreseeability determine whether a naturally-occurring event will amount to an intervening act which breaks the chain of causation. In the example above, a freak wave is an unpredictable event so it is likely to be unforeseeable and amount to an intervening act. Compare this to a situation in which an unconscious victim is left below the tide line and drowns when the tide comes in. This is a wholly foreseeable occurrence so it will not break the chain of causation. Even though the defendant did not drown the victim directly, he put the victim in a position where it was foreseeable that the victim would drown so liability would be established.

■ Omissions

Liability for omission is only necessary if there is no culpable positive act. Always base liability on what the defendant *has done*, if possible, rather than what he *has not done*.

The general rule is that there is no liability in criminal law for omissions. There are exceptions to that rule if there is a duty to act. Such a duty can arise in various ways:

Statute

A duty to act is an onerous burden that is only imposed by statute in a narrow range of circumstances, generally requiring action in situations where inaction would be unreasonable. For example, s.170(4) of the Road Traffic Act 1988 imposes a duty upon a driver involved in an accident to report it to the police or provide his details to other parties involved.

Contract

If a person fails to do something they are bound by contract to do, they will be criminally liable if harm or injury arises from their omission even though the person harmed was not a party to the contract.

R v. *Pittwood* (1902) 19 TLR 37

Concerning: duty to act, contract

Facts

The defendant was contracted to open and close level-crossing gates to ensure that nobody was harmed by the trains. He failed to close the gates and the victim was killed by a train.

Legal principle

A person under contract will be liable for the harmful consequences of his failure to perform his contractual obligations. This duty extends to those reasonably affected by the omission, not just the other party to the contract.

EXAM TIP

If a problem question involves someone with a particular job, consider what it is that his contract will oblige him to do and whether his failure to do this contributed to death.

Special relationships

Certain relationships can create a duty to act, for example, parent/child, husband/wife and doctor/patient. These are relationships where there is dependence, reliance and responsibility; for example, in *Gibbins and Proctor* (1918) 13 Cr App R 134, the first defendant failed to provide food for his child who starved to death. His liability was based upon his omission to fulfil the duty established by the special relationship of father/child.

Voluntary assumption of care

The second defendant in *Gibbins and Proctor* was the partner of the child's father. She was also liable for her omission to provide food but liability was based not on the nature of the relationship but because she had previously fed the child but had ceased to do so. A person cannot cast off the duty to act that the voluntary assumption of care imposes.

Dangerous situations

The categories of duty are based on common principles of knowledge (that the victim is in need) and reliance (the victim relies upon the defendant for help; the rest of the world relies upon the defendant to be responsible thus precluding their intervention). It is these principles which lead to the expansion of the situations in which there is a duty to act, to include the creation of a dangerous situation.

Further expansion?

This extension of the categories of duty in *Miller* left the door open for further expansion. In *Khan* [1998] Crim LR 830, consideration was given to whether a drug-dealer whose 'customer' had collapsed following self-administration of drugs was under a duty to act by summoning medical assistance. However, this could be seen as the application of the *Miller* principle rather than a new category of duty.

Chapter summary:
Putting it all together

Answer to sample question

See the problem question at the start of the chapter. A diagram illustrating how to structure your answer is available on the website.

Points to remember when answering this question
- Causation is a two-stage process so establish both factual and legal causation.
- Start by considering the liability of the primary party (Darius) and consider whether any of the other parties have broken the chain of causation.
- Having reached a conclusion in relation to Darius, go on to consider whether any of the parties would incur criminal liability too: remember that more than one person can be liable for causing the death of a single victim.
- Incorporate references to case law, remembering that the legal principle is more important than the facts of the case.
- Reach a conclusion that summarises your findings rather than ending your answer after a discussion of the last party's liability without drawing the strands of your answer together.

Make your answer really stand out
Problem questions involving causation typically involve several parties who have contributed, to a greater or lesser degree, to the end result (typically the death of the victim). The ability to create a well-organised answer that deals with each party in a methodical manner will draw attention to your problem-solving skills and help you to present a clear picture of each party's liability. A timeline of events that identifies each

party's contribution (which can be found on the companion website) may help you do this by giving you a clear picture of the order of events to work from when preparing your answer. Remember that credit is available for the way that questions are answered, as well as for legal content, so it is worth spending some time planning the structure of your answer.

3
Mens rea

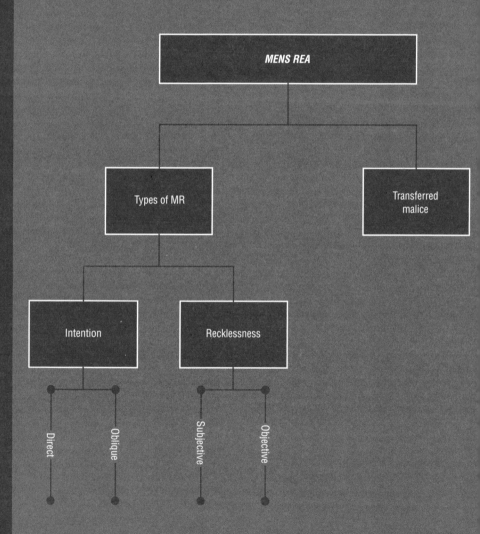

Revision checklist

What you need to know:

- [ ] The types of *mens rea* and their role in establishing liability
- [ ] The distinction between direct and oblique intention
- [ ] The distinction between subjective and objective recklessness
- [ ] The current tests on intention and recklessness to be applied in problem scenarios
- [ ] The evolution of the current law on intention and recklessness
- [ ] The operation of transferred malice

Introduction:
Understanding *mens rea*

Mens rea refers to the guilty mind required for criminal liability.

This chapter concentrates on intention and recklessness as these forms of *mens rea* are part of most offences and have been the subject of judicial scrutiny. The volume of case law on intention and recklessness can seem daunting but this demonstrates the problems the courts have had in perfecting an appropriate definition.

The judicial approach to intention and recklessness can be tricky to grasp. *Mens rea* is concerned with the defendant's state of mind at the time of the *actus reus*. It is difficult to prove what was in someone's mind which partially explains why the courts struggled with these words. Remember that the words have a *legal meaning*. Students often struggle because intention in law can mean something different to its ordinary meaning. Accept that this is the result of judicial interpretation of the words and that legal and dictionary definitions do not always match.

Essay question advice

Essays require either *broad* general knowledge of the types of *mens rea*, their relationship to each other and their role in ascribing criminal liability or they will take a *narrow* focus, requiring an examination of a particular type of *mens rea*, such as the difficulty of defining oblique intention. Either type of question requires understanding of the development of the law, i.e. earlier cases as well as the current law.

Problem question advice

Problems involving *mens rea* always involve substantive offences, often murder (intention) and non-fatal offences and criminal damage (recklessness). Problems raising issues of recklessness are particularly likely following *R* v. *G* [2003] 4 All ER 765. Stick to the current tests for intention or recklessness in problem questions – there is no place for a discussion of the evolution of the law.

Sample question

Could you answer this question? Below is a typical problem question that could arise on this topic. Guidelines on answering the question are included at the end of the chapter, whilst a sample essay question and guidance on tackling it can be found on the companion website.

Problem question

Donald cuts the brakes on Andrew's car, hoping that this will frighten him into repaying the £5000 that he owes. Andrew's wife, Vera, borrows the car and is killed when the brakes fail and the car crashes into a brick wall.

Discuss Donald's liability for murder and criminal damage.

■ Types of *mens rea*

Intention is the most culpable form of *mens rea*. This is because it is more blameworthy to cause harm deliberately (intention) than it is to do so carelessly (recklessness). Therefore, intention is used in more serious offences: murder requires intention to kill or cause GBH which sets it apart from other, less culpable, forms of homicide.

Intention

Direct intention

KEY DEFINITION

Direct intention corresponds with the everyday meaning of intention. A person who has causing death as his aim, purpose or goal has direct intention to kill.

It was defined in *Mohan* [1975] 2 All ER 193 as 'a decision to bring about... the commission of an offence... no matter whether the defendant desired the consequences of his act or not'.

Oblique intention

This is broader than **direct intention** and includes the foreseeable and inescapable consequences of achieving a desired result, even if the consequence itself is not desired.

Problem area: oblique intention

Students tend to find oblique intention difficult, probably because it differs from the ordinary meaning of intention, being a broader concept. It may help to think about the reason that the courts expanded the definition of intention – to widen the net to catch more defendants, particularly in relation to murder. As murder has no alternative *mens rea* of recklessness, defendants cannot be liable unless they fall within the scope of intention. If this is limited to direct intention, a defendant would only be liable if his purpose was to cause death. A defendant who caused death in pursuit of some other end would not be liable for murder even if achieving his primary purpose rendered death inevitable.

For example, if the defendant wants to destroy a package on an aeroplane to collect the insurance, he would not be liable for murder if he planted a bomb timed to go off in mid-flight unless the definition of intention went beyond direct intention.

Formulating a definition which captured the appropriate level of fault proved difficult. The courts tried on several occasions, only to have their definition revised by subsequent courts. The challenge was producing a test that was sufficiently narrow so as to reserve liability for murder to only the most serious manifestations of homicide. The matter is largely decided since *Woollin* but awareness of the journey to this point is essential (see Figure 3.1).

Figure 3.1

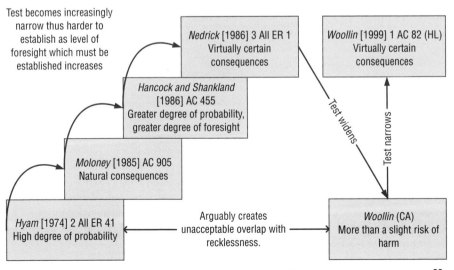

Test becomes increasingly narrow thus harder to establish as level of foresight which must be established increases

Nedrick [1986] 3 All ER 1
Virtually certain consequences

Woollin [1999] 1 AC 82 (HL)
Virtually certain consequences

Hancock and Shankland [1986] AC 455
Greater degree of probability, greater degree of foresight

Moloney [1985] AC 905
Natural consequences

Hyam [1974] 2 All ER 41
High degree of probability

Arguably creates unacceptable overlap with recklessness.

Woollin (CA)
More than a slight risk of harm

Test widens

Test narrows

The cases shown in Figure 3.1 aimed to formulate a test that conveyed an appropriate degree of inevitability:

- *Moloney* (HL): used 'natural consequences' to describe something that necessarily followed the defendant's pursuit of his primary purpose. This was ambiguous as natural consequences need not be inevitable: pregnancy is a natural consequence of intercourse but it is by no means inevitable.
- *Hancock and Shankland* (HL): addressed this ambiguity, stating that reference should be made to the degree of probability that the prohibited outcome would result from the defendant achieving his primary purpose. Their reasoning was as shown in Figure 3.2.

Figure 3.2

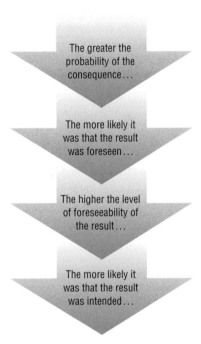

- *Moloney* and *Hancock and Shankland* conflicted in their formulation of an appropriate test of oblique intention.
- *Nedrick* (CA): addressed the conflict and formulated the *virtual certainty* test which conveyed inevitability (*Moloney*) and foreseeability (*Hancock and Shankland*).
- As *Nedrick* lacked the authoritative status of a House of Lords decision, subsequent case law eroded the narrow virtual certainty test. Ultimately, the Court of Appeal in *Woollin* accepted a test based upon 'substantial risk' which created a dangerous overlap with recklessness (therefore blurring the line between murder and manslaughter).
- *Woollin* (HL): reversed the CA decision, restored the virtual certainty test and set to rest much of the uncertainty.

R v. *Woollin* [1998] 3 WLR 382

Concerning: oblique intention, virtual certainty

Facts

The defendant threw his baby in exasperation when it would not stop crying. The baby died from head injuries. It was accepted that the defendant did not intend to cause harm to the child. His conviction for murder was upheld by the Court of Appeal on the basis that it was not a misdirection to explain oblique intention to the jury in terms of 'appreciation of a substantial risk of injury'. His appeal was allowed by the House of Lords.

Legal principle

The appropriate test for oblique intention was that formulated in *Nedrick*. A jury may find that a defendant intended an outcome if it was a virtually certain consequence of his actions and he realised this was the case.

FURTHER THINKING

An essay on oblique intention must demonstrate understanding of the progression of the case law. These articles provide clear outlines of the cases and the underlying policy issues in detail that is beyond the scope of this revision guide:

- Norrie, A., 'After *Woollin*' [1999] *Criminal Law Review* 532
- Simister, A.P. and Chan, W., 'Intention Thus Far' [1997] *Criminal Law Review* 740

EXAM TIP

An ability to distinguish direct and oblique intention is crucial. Try answering the following questions to identify the type of intention:

1 *What was the defendant trying to achieve?* If the answer is 'death' then it is an issue of direct intention and it should be straightforward to establish liability for murder (this may lead to issues of voluntary manslaughter, Chapter 7). If the answer is 'something other than death', turn to oblique intention.
2 *Was death an inevitable consequence of achieving his primary purpose?* If so, this is likely to be oblique intention so apply the 'virtual certainty' test from *Woollin*. If you are not sure, think about whether the facts suggest that the defendant must have seen death 'out of the corner of his eye' when embarking on his primary objective as this also points towards oblique intention.

If the facts raise neither direct nor oblique intention but the defendant caused death, the issue becomes involuntary manslaughter (Chapter 8).

Recklessness

Recklessness is a less culpable form of *mens rea* based upon unjustified risk-taking. The law on recklessness has been subject to change over the years as the courts have fluctuated between a subjective and objective approach.

Until *R* v. *G*, subjective and objective recklessness operated side-by-side with *Caldwell* (objective) recklessness applying to criminal damage and *Cunningham* (subjective) recklessness applying to all other offences involving an element of recklessness.

The House of Lords decision in *R* v. *G* resolved some of the difficulties inherent in a dual standard of recklessness by overruling *Caldwell* and removing objective recklessness from criminal law. However, they replaced *Caldwell* with a subjective test that differs from *Cunningham* so there are still two types of recklessness in operation.

EXAM TIP

Make sure that you have grasped the sphere of operation of the two forms of recklessness. Remember that *R* v. *G* replaces *Caldwell* so applies only to criminal damage whilst *Cunningham* (often in a modified form) applies to all other offences involving recklessness. It is a common mistake to say that *R* v. *G* replaces all previous tests of recklessness.

KEY CASE

R v. *G* [2004] 1 AC 1034

Concerning: recklessness, criminal damage

Facts

Two boys (11 and 12) set fire to a bin outside a supermarket during the night. The fire spread, destroying the supermarket. They were convicted of criminal damage following application of objective *Caldwell* recklessness despite the fact that their youth and inexperience prevented them from recognising the risk of the fire spreading and property being damaged.

Legal principle

The House of Lords overruled *Caldwell* because it imposed liability upon those who were incapable, through no fault of their own, of operating at the standards of the reasonable man. They formulated a subjective test based upon the Draft Criminal Code:

A person acts recklessly within the meaning of section 1 of the Criminal Damage Act 1971 with respect to-

(i) a circumstance when he is aware of a risk that it exists or will exist;
(ii) a result when he is aware of a risk that it will occur;

and it is, in the circumstances known to him, unreasonable to take the risk.

FURTHER THINKING

A good grasp of the problems of the pre-*R* v. *G* position, the ruling in *R* v. *G* and the reasons for it are essential for success in an essay on recklessness.

Consider the following justifications for Lord Bingham's ruling:

1 Criminal liability for serious offences should be based upon culpability; this requires a guilty mind as well as a guilty act. Failing to appreciate an obvious risk through no fault of one's own is not a sufficiently culpable state of mind.

2 *Caldwell* applied a common standard of foresight (the reasonable man) that did not take account of an individual's ability to operate at that level. This created manifest injustice to the young and those with mental disabilities who were incapable of operating at this standard.

3 There was a strong dissenting voice in *Caldwell* and it has since attracted widespread judicial and academic criticism.

Do you understand the impact of *R* v. *G* and the difference that it makes to liability for criminal damage?

Consider *Elliot* v. *C* [1983] 1 WLR 939. A 14-year-old girl with learning difficulties was out at night. She sheltered in a shed and lit a fire for warmth, using white spirit. The shed was destroyed in the ensuing blaze.

Make sure that you understand how the case *was* decided using *Caldwell* recklessness and how it *would be* decided now following *R* v. *G*. Which outcome do you consider to be preferable?

Caldwell (objective) recklessness	*R* v. *G* (subjective) recklessness
Test: did the defendant create an obvious and serious risk that property would be damaged or destroyed. If so, did he fail to recognise a risk that would have been obvious to the reasonable man?	*Test*: was the defendant aware of a risk of the damage/destruction of property and, in the circumstances, was it unreasonable for her to take that risk?
The risk of damage from an out-of-control fire would be obvious to the reasonable man. As such, the defendant failed to recognise an obvious risk and thus falls within the remit of *Caldwell* recklessness and was convicted of criminal damage. This position was heavily criticised and contributed to the demise of *Caldwell* recklessness.	This test is subjective so focuses on what this particular defendant knew and expected to result from her actions. As the defendant was young with learning difficulties, it may well be that she was unable to recognise the risks posed by her actions. If so, she would not be reckless and thus would not be liable for criminal damage.

> **EXAM TIP**
>
> *R* v. *G* formulates a test of subjective recklessness that differs from *Cunningham* subjective recklessness. Therefore the law has moved from having one objective and one subjective test (*Caldwell* and *Cunningham*) to having two subjective tests (*R* v. *G* and *Cunningham*).

█ Transferred malice

Transferred malice is a means of imposing liability for the unplanned consequences of deliberate wrongdoing. If the defendant has the *mens rea* of murder in relation to A but brings about the *actus reus*, i.e. causes death, in relation to B he may still be liable. Transferred malice only operates if the *actus reus* of the offence committed matches the *actus reus* of the offence planned.

Pembliton (1874) LR CCR 119 and *Latimer* (1886) 17 QBD 359 illustrate the principle in operation (Figure 3.3).

Figure 3.3

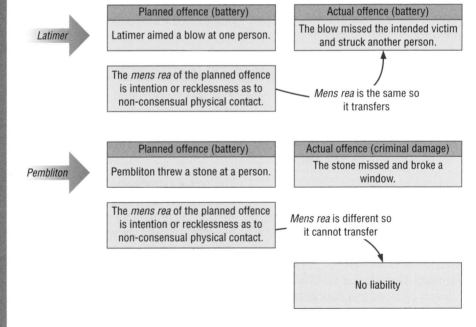

Chapter summary:
Putting it all together

☐ Can you tick all the points from the revision checklist at the beginning of this chapter?

☐ Take the **end-of-chapter quiz** on the companion website.

☐ Test your knowledge of the cases with the **revision flashcards** on the website.

☐ Attempt the problem question from the beginning of the chapter using the guidelines below.

☐ Go to the companion website to try out other questions.

Answer guidelines

See the problem question at the start of the chapter. A diagram illustrating how to structure your answer is available on the website.

Points to remember when answering this question

■ Start with the most serious offence. Vera is dead so focus on murder before discussing criminal damage.

■ Follow the instructions in the question: there is no need to discuss manslaughter.

■ Shorter questions tend to involve fewer issues therefore greater detail is required. Make sure you are confident that you have sufficient knowledge of the key issues before attempting the question.

■ Concentrate on the problem areas. The focus is on *mens rea* so avoid excessive discussion of *actus reus* issues.

■ Use transferred malice where appropriate if the planned *actus reus* and the actual *actus reus* match.

Make your answer really stand out
Avoiding common errors such as:

■ applying the wrong test of *mens rea* for the offence or the circumstances; and,

■ providing too much background detail when answering a problem question.

In a question of this nature, students often got confused about which type of *mens rea* applies. Remember two simple rules to avoid this mistake:

1 In relation to intention, firstly apply direct intention. If it is inapplicable, move to the virtual certainty test to establish oblique intention.

2 If the offence involves recklessness, apply *R* v. *G* to criminal damage only and *Cunningham* to all other offences.

By following this, you should always apply the correct *mens rea* for the offence.

Also, remember only to state the current law and apply it to the facts when answering problem questions. There is no place for a discussion of the way that the law developed or the controversy surrounding a particular test. These issues belong in essays so to include them in a problem answer weakens your focus and carries no marks at all so should be avoided.

4
Inchoate offences

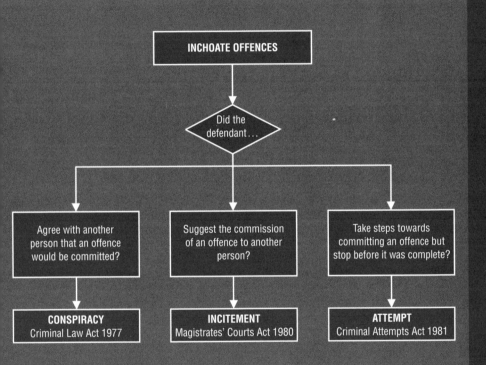

INCHOATE OFFENCES

Did the defendant…

Agree with another person that an offence would be committed?

Suggest the commission of an offence to another person?

Take steps towards committing an offence but stop before it was complete?

CONSPIRACY
Criminal Law Act 1977

INCITEMENT
Magistrates' Courts Act 1980

ATTEMPT
Criminal Attempts Act 1981

Revision checklist

What you need to know:

- [ ] The *actus reus* and *mens rea* of the three inchoate offences
- [ ] Why liability is imposed for inchoate offences
- [ ] The relationship between conspiracy and incitement
- [ ] The meaning of 'more than merely preparatory'

Introduction:
Understanding inchoate offences

Inchoate means incomplete or unfinished.

Inchoate offences are a means of imposing liability on a defendant who started to take steps towards the commission of an offence but stopped before the offence was complete. For example:

- *conspiracy* criminalises the planning stage at which defendants agree to commit an offence;
- *incitement* imposes liability on those who encourage others to commit offences whilst not taking an active part themselves; and,
- *attempt* penalises thwarted or abandoned efforts to complete an offence.

The key to understanding inchoate offences is to think about why they exist at all. What is the law trying to achieve when it imposes liability on those who have not actually brought about the *actus reus* of an offence? By addressing the rationale for their existence, inchoate offences become more explicable. Think also about whether you agree with their existence. Should a person who agreed to commit an offence be liable for conspiracy to commit that offence if he decides not to go ahead? Try to incorporate notions of 'harm i nto your thoughts about inchoate offences by considering why the preliminary stages that precede the actual offence are harmful.

Essays on inchoate offences often cover the justification for imposing liability on defendants who have stopped short of committing an offence. An answer should address the rationale fo the existence of inchoate offences in general and then consider the rationale for each of the inchoate offences. It is useful to be able to answer the question 'why' about each of these: why do we have inchoate offences, why do we criminalise conspiracy, incitement and attempt.

Problem questions usually involve inchoate offences in combination with substantive offences. It is because they could combine with *any* other offence or defence that it is essential that you can spot inchoate offences and deal with them effectively. Remember that conspiracy and incitement involves two parties so cannot arise in problems with only one defendant. Attempt does not require collaboration so can arise with a single defendant.

Sample question

Could you answer this question? Below is a typical problem question that could arise on this topic. Guidelines on answering the question are included at the end of the chapter, whilst a sample essay question and guidance on tackling it can be found on the companion website.

Alfred tells Bernard and Charles that he wishes that Victor was dead. Bernard and Charles later agree to kill Victor to gain favour with Alfred. They agree to meet at 8pm to carry out the murder. Charles does not turn up as planned so Bernard takes an axe and goes to wait in an alley outside Victor's house. By 10pm, Victor has not appeared so Bernard gives up and goes home.

Discuss the criminal liability of Alfred, Bernard and Charles.

▮ Conspiracy

There are two types of conspiracy with different sets of rules:

1 common law conspiracy (to defraud, to corrupt public morals)
2 statutory conspiracy (to commit any other offence).

This chapter deals with statutory conspiracy.

KEY STATUTORY PROVISION

Criminal Law Act 1977, s.1(1)

If a person agrees with any other person or persons that a course of conduct shall be pursued which, if the agreement is carried out in accordance with their intentions, either

(a) will necessarily amount to or involve the commission of any offence or offences by one or more of the parties to the agreement; or,

(b) would do so but for the existence of facts which render the commission of the offence or any of the offences impossible,

he is guilty of conspiracy to commit the offence or offences in question.

Three *actus reus* elements	Two *mens rea* elements
agreement	intention to carry out agreed course of conduct
between the parties	intention to commit the substantive offence
specified course of conduct	

Actus reus elements

Agreement

Agreement is the essence of conspiracy. The parties need not commit the agreed offence or take steps towards doing so as their liability is complete once the agreement is reached.

The agreement need only be general. If the parties have agreed to kill someone it is irrelevant that they have not yet decided when or how they will carry out the murder.

The parties

Conspiracy requires at least two people (a person cannot conspire alone!). Certain categories of people are excluded from this calculation:

■ husband and wife: s.2(2)(a)
■ those under the age of criminal responsibility: s.2(2)(b)
■ the intended victim: s.2(2)(c).

A person may conspire with 'person or persons unknown' if the identity of the other parties is not known. Therefore, a single defendant can be convicted of conspiracy if others are unidentified or have been acquitted.

Course of conduct

The course of conduct agreed between the parties must be one that would necessarily amount to an offence by one of the conspirators if the plan was carried to fruition. Focus on what the conspirators plan to do even if their plans are conditional on the circumstances being favourable.

KEY CASE

R v. Jackson [1985] Crim LR 442

Concerning: conspiracy, contingent plans

Facts

The defendant and another agreed to shoot a third man in the leg if he was convicted of an offence for which he was on trial so that he would attract leniency in sentencing. The defendant appealed against his conviction for conspiracy to pervert the course of justice because he had planned to do something that might never happen (there would be no need to shoot the third party if he was acquitted).

Legal principle

The Court of Appeal rejected this argument and held that a contingent plan to commit an offence was still a plan to commit an offence if it was necessary (or possible).

Consider the 'best case scenario' of the conspirators to determine what they plan to achieve. If their plan would be a failure without achieving this aim then this is what they have conspired to achieve. For example:

Facts	Liability
Alison and Brenda have no money. They decide to steal a gift for their mother from a shop if it is so busy that they can do so without being spotted.	The parties will be liable for conspiracy to steal despite the contingent nature of their plan. If their plan is successful, they will have committed theft so they are liable for conspiracy to commit theft even though the shop may not be sufficiently busy for them to go ahead with their plan.

Mens rea elements

Both aspects of the *mens rea* of conspiracy are based on the intentions of the conspirators. They must *intend* to agree to commit an offence and *intend* that their course of conduct will lead to this offence. It is not necessary for all the conspirators to participate in the planned offence provided at least one of them does so.

■ Incitement

Incitement criminalises the actions of those who are instrumental in causing others to offend. It aims to prevent people from avoiding liability by getting others to commit offences for them.

The elements of incitement are straightforward but it has complex procedural elements. The Magistrates' Court Act 1980 provides that whether the defendant is charged a summary or indictable offence will depend upon the nature of the offence incited. In essence, the seriousness of incitement relates to the seriousness of the offence incited: for instance, it is more serious to incite rape than it is to incite battery.

Actus reus of incitement

As a common law offence, there is no statutory definition of incitement so its principles must be distilled from case law.

KEY DEFINITION

Incitement *Goldman* [1997] Crim LR 894 held that a person who incites 'reaches and seeks to influence the mind of another to the commission of a crime' and that this can take the following forms:

suggestion	proposals	request
exhortation	gesture	argument
persuasion	inducement	goading

This list reveals that incitement can take many forms, ranging from suggestion to compulsion. Case law provides further insight into the nature of incitement:

■ It is not enough to advise another of an opportunity to commit an offence; there must be positive encouragement (*Hendrickson and Tichner* [1977] Crim LR 356).
■ The level of encouragement required is law. Saying 'oh goody' upon hearing an offence is planned will suffice (*Gianetto* (1997) 1 Cr App R 1).
■ Incitement will be established even if the recipient would have committed the offence without encouragement (*Goldman* [1997] Crim LR 894) or is not persuaded to commit the offence at all (*Marlow* [1998] 1 Cr App R (S) 273).
■ Incitement can be implied, e.g. publication of a book on cultivation of cannabis as incitement to commit a drugs offence (*Marlow*).

- A person may incite the world at large as well as specific individuals, e.g. advertisement of a speed-trap detector in a magazine was incitement to the world at large: *Invicta Plastics* v. *Clare* [1976] RTR 251.

Mens rea of incitement

There has been confusion in case law concerning the *mens rea* of incitement that has now been resolved:

KEY CASE

DPP v. *Armstrong* [2000] Crim LR 379

Concerning: incitement, *mens rea*

Facts

The defendant asked another man to supply child pornography, not realising that the recipient of his request was a police officer. He was acquitted of inciting the supply of child pornography at first instance as he argued that the officer had no intention of supplying the material despite having access to it through his work (i.e. the officer lacked the *mens rea* for the substantive offence). The prosecution appealed by way of case stated and the Divisional Court ruled that the *parity of mens rea* principle from *Curr* and *Shaw* was incorrect.

Legal principle

The *mens rea* of incitement must be established only by reference to the defendant's state of mind and required that the defendant *intended* to incite another to commit an offence. No consideration should be given to the incitee's state of mind when determining the inciter's liability; it was irrelevant whether the incitee was influenced by the incitement provided that the inciter intended that he would be influenced.

FURTHER THINKING

The *mens rea* of incitement has caused difficulties for the courts so would make a useful focus for discussion in an essay that invites a critique of inchoate offences. Reference to any issues that have puzzled the courts can be a good way to make your answer stand out. A useful article which explores the complexity of the *mens rea* of incitement is Alexander, L. and Kessler, D., '*Mens Rea* and Inchoate Crimes' (1997) *Journal of Criminal Law and Criminology* 1138.

▮Attempt

Liability for attempt is governed by the Criminal Attempts Act 1981. This covers attempts to commit indictable offences only; it is not an offence to attempt a summary offence, e.g. there is no offence of attempted battery.

<table>
<tr><td rowspan="2">KEY STATUTORY PROVISION</td><td>**Criminal Attempts Act 1981, s.1(1)**</td></tr>
<tr><td>If, with intent to commit an offence to which this section applies, a person does an act which is more than merely preparatory to the commission of the offence, he is guilty of attempting to commit the offence.</td></tr>
</table>

Two *actus reus* elements	The *mens rea* element
an act (not omission)	intention to commit the substantive offence
which is more than merely preparatory to the commission of an offence	

Actus reus elements

More than merely preparatory

Liability for attempt is based upon a demarcation between planning/preparation (not an offence) and embarkation on an active endeavour to commit an offence (attempt) that stops short of the substantive offence (substantive liability). This is demonstrated in Figure 4.1.

Attempt requires that the defendant has done something *more than merely preparatory*. Movement between these stages will depend on the nature of the substantive offence as some offences require more planning and preparation than others.

Think about the steps towards committing a robbery. At what stage would Dennis incur liability for attempted robbery?

■ Dennis decides to rob a bank.
■ He visits it to familiarise himself with the layout of the building.
■ He purchases a balaclava and gloves.

Figure 4.1

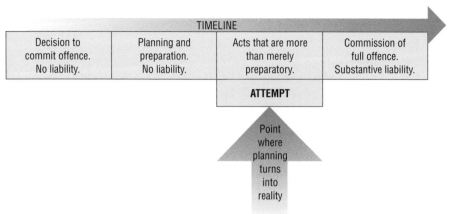

- He acquires and modifies a shotgun.
- He steals a car to use as a getaway vehicle.
- He drives to the bank.
- He goes into the bank and approaches the counter.
- He points the shotgun at the cashier.
- He passes the cashier a note demanding money.

It is easy to dismiss some of these stages as planning and preparation, but is it straightforward to decide at which stage the defendant's conduct becomes more than merely preparatory?

Problem area: more than merely preparatory

The courts have not always taken a consistent approach to 'more than merely preparatory'. The initial test was *proximity* between the defendant's act and the completed offence. This required that the defendant had completed the final act of preparation: having 'crossed the Rubicon and burned his boats' (*Stonehouse* [1978] AC 55). This restricted liability for attempt. For example, a jeweller who faked a burglary was not liable for attempting to make a fraudulent insurance claim because he had not obtained and completed a claim form (*Robinson* [1915] 2 KB 342).

Case law after the enactment of the Criminal Attempts Act 1981 has placed less emphasis on proximity leading to a broadening of liability for attempt.

R v. Griffen [1993] Crim LR 515

Concerning: more than merely preparatory

Facts

The defendant planned to remove her children from the custody of their father. She booked ferry tickets and told the school that she would collect the children to take them to the dentist. Her conviction for attempting to abduct the children was upheld even though she was apprehended before she collected the children from school.

R v. Geddes [1996] Crim LR 894

Facts

The defendant was in school toilets without lawful reason with masking tape and a knife in his possession. His conviction for attempting to falsely imprison a child was overturned as he had not moved beyond preparation; he was in a position where he *could* commit the offence but he had not started to do so. As he had not approached a child, he had not 'moved from the realm of intention, preparation and planning into... execution and implementation'.

Legal principle

'More than merely preparatory' is characterised not by physical conduct but in a psychological commitment to the commission of the substantive offence. The defendant in *Geddes* may not have continued to complete the substantive offences despite having put himself in a position where he could do so whereas the defendant in *Griffen* had no such ambiguity of commitment to carrying the substantive offence to fruition; she was implementing her plan but was interrupted before its completion.

The cases may seem inconsistent as the defendant in *Geddes* was within reach of children but not liable whilst the defendant in *Griffen* was liable despite not being anywhere near her children. However, they demonstrate the shift from the 'final act' proximity approach to a focus on the psychological commitment of the defendant to completing the offence.

Mens rea of attempt

The *mens rea* of attempt is variable because it is an intention to commit the substantive offence: a defendant charged with attempted robbery must have intended to commit robbery whilst a defendant charged with attempted rape must have intended to commit rape.

This remains true even if the substantive offence can be committed recklessly. For example, criminal damage requires *either* intention *or* recklessness (to destroy/damage property belonging to another: Chapter 12) but intention to damage/destroy another's property is required for attempted criminal damage.

Problem area: attempted murder ·

The *mens rea* for murder is intention to kill or cause GBH (Chapter 6) but the *mens rea* for attempted murder is limited to intention to kill. This is because an attempted offence involves a failed outcome, i.e. the victim is not dead. If the victim is alive and the defendant only intended to cause GBH, he is liable for a non-fatal offence (Chapter 10); he cannot be liable for attempted murder unless he intended to kill the victim.

EXAM TIP

The *actus reus* of attempt is directly referable to the *actus reus* of the substantive offence. Therefore, the 'more than merely preparatory' conduct will vary according to the nature of the substantive offence that the defendant has attempted. The *mens rea* of attempt is not referable to the substantive offence; it remains consistent as an intention to commit the substantive offence irrespective of the type of offence or its *mens rea*.

Chapter summary:
Putting it all together

- [ ] Can you tick all the points from the revision checklist at the beginning of this chapter?
- [ ] Take the **end-of-chapter quiz** on the companion website.
- [ ] Test your knowledge of the cases with the **revision flashcards** on the website.
- [ ] Attempt the problem question from the beginning of the chapter using the guidelines below.
- [ ] Go to the companion website to try out other questions.

Answer guidelines

See the problem question at the start of the chapter. A diagram illustrating how to structure your answer is available on the website.

Points to remember when answering this question
- Deal with each party separately and work through liability in a methodical manner.
- It can be useful to think of events chronologically.
- If there is no clear consequence, do not be misled into assuming there is no liability. Absence of concrete consequences is a sign that the parties are likely to have incurred inchoate liability.
- Associate key words with each of the offences: conspiracy–agreement, incitement–encouragement, attempt–beyond preparation.

Make your answer really stand out
Present a clear, well-structured answer however tangled the facts are in the problem. Preparation is the key to clarity. Plan your answer based upon the facts, issues and arguments for and against liability as demonstrated below and reach a balanced conclusion.

	Alfred	Bernard	Charles
Facts	A tells B and C he wishes V was dead.	B and C plan to kill V.	C waits for V with an axe, planning to kill him.
Issues	Does this statement amount to incitement to murder?	Does this amount to conspiracy to kill?	Is this a more than merely preparatory act giving rise to attempted murder?
For liability	A placed the idea of killing V in B and C's heads. They agree to 'gain favour' with A.	If neither B or C are excluded parties, they will be liable as they have agreed a plan that will result in an offence (murder).	C has taken steps towards the planned offence (arming himself and lying in wait). If this is 'more than merely preparatory' he will be liable.
Against liability	Incitement requires more than a statement of desire. A wishes V dead but has done nothing to persuade B and C to kill V.	If either party did not intend the agreement to be acted upon, there will be no liability. B's failure to turn up may be indicative of this.	The ease with which C abandons his plan indicates lack of psychological commitment to it.
Conclusion	Absence of encouragement, likely to be statement of desire, no liability.	Evidence of agreement at the time thus liability is likely.	So much more needed to be done and C lacks commitment to carrying plan to fruition. No liability.

5
Accessorial liability

TYPES OF COLLABORATION	
JOINT PRINCIPALS Usual AR and MR for substantive offence	**PRINCIPAL AND ACCESSORY** Accessories and Abettors Act 1861, s.8

WITHDRAWAL FROM PARTICIPATION			
Level of participation	Nearness to completion	Spontaneous and planned offences	Communication of withdrawal

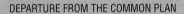

DEPARTURE FROM THE COMMON PLAN
Joint liability for consequences of plan Propensity of weapon to cause harm Relative dangerousness of weapons used

Revision checklist

What you need to know:

- [ ] Distinction between joint principals and principal/accessories
- [ ] Meaning of 'aid, abet, counsel and procure'
- [ ] Intention and knowledge required by an accessory
- [ ] Steps needed for effective withdrawal
- [ ] Consequences of departure from a common plan

Introduction:
Understanding accessorial liability

Not everyone involved in the commission of a crime plays an active part in the *actus reus*.

Accessorial liability recognises the contribution of 'behind the scenes' assistance, such as provision of weapons, advice or moral support, and penalises those who play an indirect role in the complete offence.

It is important be able to establish liability of those who play a peripheral part in the commission of an offence and to understand how and why the law imposes liability of these 'supporting actors'.

Essay question advice

Accessorial liability is a relatively unsettled area of law and thus a fertile area for essay questions. Despite this, such questions are not common, possibly due to the complexity of the issues raised by the case law. Pay particular attention to recent developments to ensure that you are well-prepared to provide an up-to-date account of the law in an essay.

Problem question advice

Problems involving accessories are easily identified as they involve several defendants. Accessorial liability can combine with any substantive offence making it a dangerous omission from revision that could seriously limit the number of questions you could answer in an exam.

Sample question

Could you answer this question? Below is a typical problem question that could arise on this topic. Guidelines on answering the question are included at the end of the chapter, whilst a sample essay question and guidance on tackling it can be found on the companion website.

Problem question

Adam finds out that Vernon has been embezzling money from their company. He tells Bernard who lends Adam a knife to 'sort him out'. Adam shows the knife to Callum and Derek, both of whom agree to accompany Adam to confront Vernon. Adam and Callum meet as agreed but Derek lost his nerve and failed to turn up. Bernard left a message for Adam saying, 'I want my knife back straight away.' Adam and Callum confront Vernon who laughs. Enraged, Adam takes out a gun and shoots Vernon, killing him outright.

Discuss the liability of the parties.

■ Types of collaboration

When two (or more) parties embark on a criminal enterprise, their liability will depend upon the extent of their involvement with the *actus reus* of the main offence (see Figure 5.1).

Figure 5.1

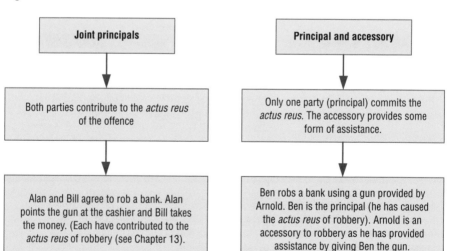

The situation is more straightforward when the parties are joint principles as both must have the *actus reus* and *mens rea* of the offence in question. Accessorial liability is based upon the assistance provided to the principal, which may take a variety of different forms. For example, Arnold assisted by providing a gun but others may have helped Ben commit the robbery: Conrad drove the getaway car, David kept look-out and Eric attacked the security guard. All these activities may give rise to accessorial liability.

Problem area: liability of principals and accessories

Clearly, accessorial liability can take many forms as there are so many different ways in which an accessory can provide assistance. The liability of the principal and accessory generally matches; for example, the principal is liable for theft and the accessory is guilty of aiding and abetting theft. There are two exceptional situations in which liability of principal and accessory differ:

∎ The principal is acquitted but the accessory remains liable

∎ The principal has a defence. In *Bourne* (1952) 36 Cr App R 125, the defendant was convicted as accessory to buggery after forcing his wife to have intercourse with a dog. She was acquitted by virtue of duress (Chapter 20).

∎ The principal lacks *mens rea*. In *DPP* v. *K and B* [1997] Cr App R 36, the defendants (girls of 14 and 11) encouraged the principal to have intercourse with the victim, a 14-year-old girl they had been holding captive by threats. They were convicted as accessories to rape despite failure to establish that the principal (who had not been identified or traced) had the *mens rea* of the rape (he may have been unaware that the victim was not consenting). He committed the *actus reus* (non-consensual intercourse) which was sufficient to found accessorial liability. This also demonstrates that a person can be an accessory to an offence they cannot commit as principal (both defendants were female – rape can only be committed by a male).

∎ Principal and accessory are liable for different offences

This may arise if offences have the same *actus reus* but different *mens rea*, e.g. OAPA, ss.18 and 20 (Chapter 10). Alternatively, the principal may have a defence that reduces his liability such as the reduction of murder to manslaughter by virtue of provocation (Chapter 7).

■ Accessorial liability

KEY STATUTORY PROVISIONS

Accessories and Abettors Act 1861, s.8

Whoever shall aid, abet, counsel or procure the commission of any indictable offence…shall be liable to be tried, indicted and punished as a principal offender.

Magistrates' Courts Act 1980, s.44

Comparable provision for summary offences.

Four *actus reus* elements	Three *mens rea* elements
Aid	Intention to do an act with knowledge that it will assist the principal
Abet	
	and
Counsel	
	Intention to assist the principal
Procure	
	and
	Knowledge of the circumstances surrounding the offence

Actus reus elements

Aid, abet, counsel and procure

KEY DEFINITIONS

Aiding, abetting, counselling, procuring In *A-G's Reference (No 1 of 1975)* [1975] QB 773, Lord Widgery stated that each word must have a different meaning otherwise Parliament would not have used four different words.

This prompted a search for distinctions in the meaning between the words with the classic statement being from Smith and Hogan (Smith, J.C. (2002) *Smith and Hogan Criminal Law*, 10th edition, London: Butterworths, pp. 145–6):

■ Procuring implies causation not consensus.
■ Abetting and counselling imply consensus not causation.
■ Aiding requires actual assistance but neither consensus nor causation.

FURTHER THINKING

Smith & Hogan's approach received judicial approval in *Able* [1984] QB 795. More recently, it was stated in *Bryce* [2004] 2 Cr App R 35 that there were shades of difference between aid, abet, counsel and procure but that all required 'some form of causal connection' between the assistance and the offence. The Court of Appeal in *Bryce* recommended that accessories should be charged using a 'catch-all' composite phrase (aid, abet, counsel or procure) to avoid acquittals based upon the difference of meaning between the words.

This difference of opinion is unresolved. In problem questions, it should suffice to identify the nature of the assistance provided by the accessory and adopt the *Bryce* recommendation of a composite phrase.

An essay question might pick up on this uncertainty so a sound understanding of the definitional debate and the departure from the accepted position in *Bryce* would be needed. It would be useful to read a case comment on *Bryce* as a means of understanding its implications in preparation for essay-writing: for example, Rees, T. and Ashworth, A., 'Aiding and Abetting: *Mens Rea* and Intention to Assist' [2004] *Criminal Law Review* 936.

Mens rea elements

The *mens rea* of accessorial liability is a combination of intention and knowledge. It was summed up in *Bryce* as having three elements (see Figure 5.2).

Figure 5.2

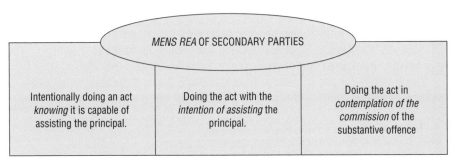

MENS REA OF SECONDARY PARTIES

Intentionally doing an act *knowing* it is capable of assisting the principal.	Doing the act with the *intention of assisting* the principal.	Doing the act in *contemplation of the commission* of the substantive offence

The first two of these requirements are summed up in the follow quotation from *Bryce*:

> 'An intention to assist (and not to hinder or obstruct) [the principal] in acts which [the accessory] knows are steps taken by [the principal] towards the commission of the offence.'

Contemplation of the offence

An accessory need not know precisely what the principal intends. He must, however, have some knowledge of the criminal purpose of the principal.

KEY CASE

R v. *Bainbridge* [1959] 3 All ER 200

Concerning: accessories, knowledge

Facts

The defendant supplied some cutting equipment suspecting it would be used for illegal purposes. He argued that he did not know the specifics of the offence, i.e. the precise location and timing of the offence.

Legal principle

It was held that knowledge that the cutting equipment was going to be used for a particular type of offence, i.e. burglary, would suffice to establish the *mens rea* of secondary liability.

The House of Lords approved this approach in *Maxwell* and extended it further:

KEY CASE

Maxwell v. *DPP for Northern Ireland* (1979) 68 Cr App R 128

Concerning: accessories, knowledge

Facts

The defendant drove people he knew to be involved in a terrorist organisation to a pub. He was unsure of exactly what they would do there but knew it would involve some sort of terrorist attack. He argued that this was insufficiently precise knowledge to render him liable as an accessory for their crimes arising from the throwing of a pipe bomb into the pub.

Legal principle

It was held that an accessory who did not know the precise nature of the offence intended by the principal would nonetheless be liable if the principal committed one of a range of possible offences that the accessory had within his contemplation.

Withdrawal from participation

Once assistance has been provided, an accessory can only avoid liability if he withdraws from the enterprise. There are several factors to take into account when considering whether there has been successful withdrawal (see Figure 5.3).

Figure 5.3

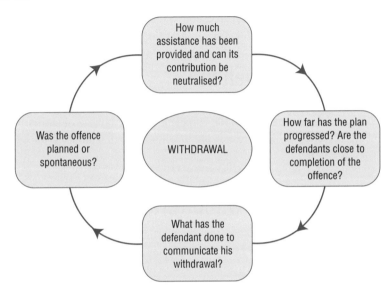

Level of participation

The rule is that the more assistance that accessory has provided, the more he must do to withdraw from the criminal enterprise.

EXAM TIP

In a problem question, balance the level of the defendant's involvement against measures he has taken to withdraw, taking into account other characteristics of effective withdrawal (below) to determine whether he has severed himself from the principal's actions.

In an essay, you may want to discuss whether it is reasonable to distinguish active assistance and passive provision of advice. The defendant in *Whitefield* provided information that enabled the burglary to be committed; nothing that he said or did, short of informing the authorities, could negate his contribution to the offence. Is it acceptable that those who provide information are more able to detach themselves from liability? The following article might help you form an opinion in preparation for an essay question: Smith, K., 'Withdrawal in Complicity: a Restatement of Principles' [2001] *Criminal Law Review* 769.

Nearness to completion

Focusing again on *Whitefield* and *Becerra*, the level of participation will often depend on the closeness of the accessory to the completion of the offence. It seems reasonable to say that the nearer events are to completion, the harder it will be for the accessory to withdraw.

Communication of withdrawal

A defendant may be able to withdraw from participation if he gives 'timely and unequivocal' notice to the other(s) that he is not going to be involved.

KEY CASE

R v. *Rook* (1993) 97 Cr App R 327

Concerning: withdrawal from participation

Facts

The defendant changed his mind about involvement in a plan to kill the wife of a friend. He failed to meet the others as planned to commit the offence.

Legal principle

The Court of Appeal held that this would not suffice to absolve the defendant of liability as he had made no attempt to communicate his withdrawal to the other parties. Accordingly, he remained liable (as there is no requirement that a person actually be present at the commission of the crime in order to attract accessorial liability).

Case law also makes it clear that it is not enough for an accessory to inform others that he is not taking part; it must be clear that he is disassociating himself from the enterprise:

R v. *Becerra* (1975) 62 Cr App R 212

Concerning: withdrawal from participation

Facts
The defendant provided a knife and went with another to commit a burglary. When they were disturbed, he jumped out of a window. The principal stabbed the householder with the defendant's knife

Legal principle
Communication of withdrawal must be timely and 'serve unequivocal notice upon the other party that if he proceeds upon it he does so without further aid and assistance of those who withdraw'.

Spontaneous and planned offences

There is less time to communicate withdrawal if an offence occurs spontaneously. In *Mitchell* [1999] Crim LR 496, it was held that the necessity of communication was waived in relation to spontaneous violence. This was discussed in *Robinson*.

R v. *Robinson* [2000] EWCA Crim 8

Concerning: withdrawal of accessories

Facts
The defendant was one of a group involved in an unplanned attack. He struck the first blow but thereafter took little part, ultimately intervening to protect the victim. The issue was whether this amounted to withdrawal.

Legal principle
This situation was characterised as a 'build-up of tension culminating in violence' rather than a truly spontaneous attack (as in *Mitchell*). A defendant who initiated an attack would only be able to withdraw in exceptional circumstances and must give unequivocal communication to others that he was withdrawing.

■ Departure from the common plan

Parties who agree to a criminal enterprise become liable for unplanned offences committed by others during the enterprise. In *Anderson and Morris* [1966] 2 QB 110, Lord Parker stated:

'Where two persons embark on a joint enterprise, each is liable for the acts done in pursuance of that joint enterprise [and]... that includes liability for unusual consequences if they arise from the execution of the agreed joint enterprise.'

EXAM TIP

The key to determining each party's liability is to work out the scope of the common plan, i.e. what the parties have agreed to do. With this in mind, consider whether what has actually happened is within this or arose directly from this.

If there is a gap, it may be that one party has departed from the common plan in a way that renders him solely liable for events that occurred.

The courts are reluctant to separate the liability of parties who embark on a criminal enterprise together. The 'liability includes unusual consequences' rule usually means all parties are equally liable. The exception to this occurs if one party has done something so different to what was agreed that it is unreasonable to hold the others responsible.

KEY CASE

R v. *Powell*; *R* v. *English* [1997] 3 WLR 959

Concerning: departure from common plan

Facts

Powell: The defendant went with others to buy drugs knowing that one of his companions was carrying a gun. The drug-dealer was shot and the defendant was convicted as accessory to murder as he was aware of the presence of the weapon thus knew its use was a possibility.
English: The defendant took part in an attack where it was agreed that fencing posts would be used to inflict injury. Another attacker produced a knife and stabbed the victim. The defendant's conviction was quashed as he was unaware of the presence of the weapon so its use was an unexpected and unforeseeable departure from the plan.

Legal principle

The House of Lords held:

1 Defendants who realised that another party *might* kill with the necessary *mens rea* during an agreed offence would be accessories to murder. Knowledge that a companion had a weapon was strong evidence that the accessory had considered the possibility that killing might occur.
2 There will be no liability as accessory to a killing caused by a weapon that the accessory did not know the principal possessed.
3 If the accessory knew that the principal had a weapon but the killing was caused by a different weapon of equal dangerousness, accessorial liability for the killing will arise.

The implications of the unexpected production of a weapon were re-examined in *Uddin* [1998] 2 All ER 744 where the questions were reframed in terms of the *propensity of the weapon to cause death* (the plan involved snooker cues but one party unexpectedly produced a knife). It was held in *Greatrex* [1999] 1 Cr App R 126 that the dangerousness of different weapons should be determined by the jury.

Following these cases, there are three possible outcomes if a principal uses a weapon when this was not part of the common plan (see Figure 5.4)

Figure 5.4

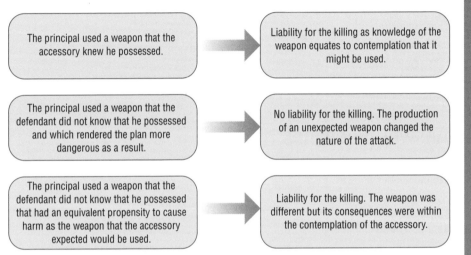

The principal used a weapon that the accessory knew he possessed.	Liability for the killing as knowledge of the weapon equates to contemplation that it might be used.
The principal used a weapon that the defendant did not know that he possessed and which rendered the plan more dangerous as a result.	No liability for the killing. The production of an unexpected weapon changed the nature of the attack.
The principal used a weapon that the defendant did not know that he possessed that had an equivalent propensity to cause harm as the weapon that the accessory expected would be used.	Liability for the killing. The weapon was different but its consequences were within the contemplation of the accessory.

EXAM TIP

In a problem question, think about the different weapons and consider whether the weapon used is (a) more, (b) less or (c) equally dangerous, compared to the weapon contemplated.

FURTHER THINKING

Question this approach to determining liability of accessories for deaths caused by others. Is relative dangerousness of weapons a useful approach or is it preferable to base liability upon knowledge of the presence of a weapon irrespective of its dangerousness? What happens, for example, if a defendant knows that another party has a gun so has contemplated that someone might be shot but the other party actually uses the gun to bludgeon the victim to death? Given that the gun was used as a blunt instrument, does this make it sufficiently different to absolve the defendant of liability? It is a difficult question.

Chapter summary:
Putting it all together

☐ Can you tick all the points from the revision checklist at the beginning of this chapter?

☐ Take the **end-of-chapter quiz** on the companion website.

☐ Test your knowledge of the cases below with the **revision flashcards** on the website.

☐ Attempt the problem question from the beginning of the chapter using the guidelines below.

☐ Go to the companion website to try out other questions.

Answer guidelines

See the problem question at the start of the chapter. A diagram illustrating how to structure your answer is available on the website.

Points to remember when answering this question

■ Untangle the facts and start with a list of what each party has done. This can be transformed into a plan which should lead to a clearly structured answer.

■ Identify the principal offender and the *actus reus* of the main offence; there can be no accessorial liability unless the substantive offence has been committed.

■ Be methodical. Establish liability first (AR and MR) then consider if it can be avoided (by withdrawal or the principal's departure from the common plan).

Make your answer really stand out

■ Incorporate case law to support your arguments using principles outlined in the key cases. For example, it was held in *Rook* that failure to turn up to commit an offence was not enough to withdraw from participation so Derek is unlikely to avoid liability on this basis.

■ Remember to present both sides of the argument. For example, Bernard's statement that he wants his knife back 'straight away' could indicate that he is revoking his involvement prior to the attack. However, the message is ambiguous. He does not urge Adam not to attack Vernon so he may just want the knife for his own purposes.

6
Murder

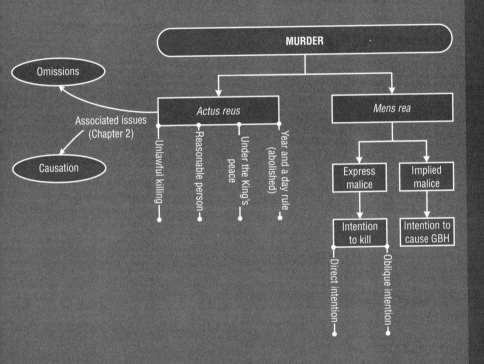

MURDER

Omissions

Associated issues
(Chapter 2)

Causation

Actus reus
- Unlawful killing
- Reasonable person
- Under the King's peace
- Year and a day rule (abolished)

Mens rea

Express malice
- Intention to kill
  - Direct intention
  - Oblique intention

Implied malice
- Intention to cause GBH

Revision checklist

What you need to know:

- [ ] *Actus reus* and *mens rea* of murder
- [ ] Role of causation and omissions
- [ ] Distinction between implied and express malice
- [ ] Scope of direct and oblique intention
- [ ] Relationship between murder and manslaughter

Introduction:
Murder

Murder is the most culpable form of homicide which carries a mandatory life sentence.

It is almost certain to feature on exam papers either as an essay topic or in a problem question (possibly both). It raises little that has not been covered in the chapters on *actus reus* and *mens rea*. It may be useful to regard this chapter as a consolidation exercise as well as touching upon points specific to murder.

Murder overlaps with voluntary and involuntary manslaughter as all homicide offences share a common *actus reus* (unlawful killing). They differ only in terms of the *mens rea* requirement.

Essay question advice

Essays tend to require engagement with underlying policy issues such as:

- relationship between murder and other homicide offences
- abolition of the murder/manslaughter distinction
- introduction of discretion in sentencing
- removal of the mandatory life sentence.

Problem question advice

Problem questions on murder often combine with other topics, particularly voluntary manslaughter (Chapter 7), involuntary manslaughter (Chapter 8) or non-fatal offences (Chapters 9 and 10) so these other topics will need thorough revision. Causation, omissions (Chapter 2) and oblique intention (Chapter 3) are common issues.

Sample question

Could you answer this question? Below is a typical problem question that could arise on this topic. Guidelines on answering the question are included at the end of the chapter, whilst a sample essay question and guidance on tackling it can be found on the companion website.

Doreen sets fire to her former employer s house. Adam, a fireman, was badly burned in the fire and kills himself a week later. Adam's wife, Deborah, decides to kill Doreen to avenge her husband's death. She shoots Maureen, Doreen's twin sister, by mistake, killing her outright.

Discuss Doreen and Deborah's liability for murder.

■ Murder

KEY DEFINITIONS

Murder Unlawfully killing any reasonable person who is in being and under the King's peace with malice aforethought where death occurs within one-year-and-a-day (Coke 3 Inst 47).

This definition has undergone some modification, as a result of case law and statutory intervention, since its inception.

Actus reus elements	Two alternative *mens rea* elements
act/omission	intention to kill (express malice)
unlawful killing	intention to cause GBH (implied malice)
reasonable person	
within King's peace	

EXAM TIP

Murder is a common law offence so its elements are found in case law. It is a common mistake to state that murder is defined in the Homicide Act 1957. This is not so. The statute deals with issues relating to homicide but does not define murder.

Actus reus of murder

The *actus reus* of murder is generally stated as unlawful killing but there are other elements to be taken into account. Note the abolition of the year-and-a-day rule (see Figure 6.1).

Figure 6.1

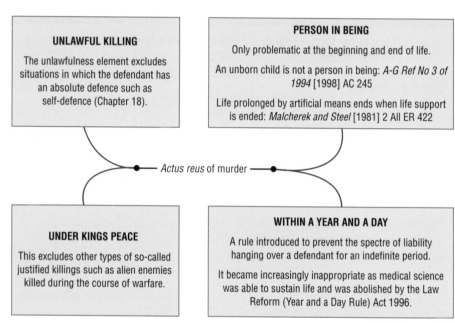

In addition to these requirements, it is essential that the defendant's act (or, in certain circumstances, omission) caused the victim's death. Causation and omissions are covered in Chapter 2, which you may like to revisit to refresh your memory.

Mens rea of murder

KEY DEFINITION

Malice aforethought Killing shall not amount to murder unless done with... malice aforethought (section 1, Homicide Act 1957). Malice aforethought was defined in *Cunningham* [1982] AC 566 as intention to kill (express malice) or cause GBH (implied malice).

The *mens rea* of murder is further broken down into two types of express malice: direct intention and oblique intention. These are covered in Chapter 3. You might like to familiarise yourself with these concepts before moving on, paying particular attention to *Woollin* [1999] 1 AC 82 (the current test for oblique intention).

There are three optional mental states in relation to murder (see also Figure 6.2):

1 Direct intention (express malice): causing death is the defendant's aim/purpose.
2 Oblique intention (express malice): death is a virtually certain consequence of the defendant's actions.
3 Implied malice: the defendant's aim is to cause GBH.

Figure 6.2

Dick decides to kill his mother. He puts poison in her coffee. The amount he used is too small to kill but his mother suffers an allergic reaction to the poison and dies anyway.	EXPRESS MALICE Direct intent	Causing death is Dick's primary intention. It does not matter that there was an extremely small chance that he would achieve this as he used such a small amount of poison.
Derek has financial problems so sets a bomb to destroy his home in order to collect the insurance. He hopes that his wife and children will escape unharmed. The blast kills all Derek's family.	EXPRESS MALICE Oblique intent	Derek's primary purpose is financial gain hence he has no direct intention to cause death. Oblique intention would be established by application of the virtual certainty test, taking into account the size and location of the bomb.
Delia wants her husband to spend more time with the family. She slices through a tendon in his leg whilst he is asleep so that he will be too injured to leave the house. He bleeds to death.	IMPLIED MALICE Intention to cause GBH	Delia's primary purpose was not to cause death neither was death a virtually certain consequence of her actions. She did intend to cause GBH so will be liable for murder even though the possibility of death arising from her actions did not occur to her.

◼Relationship with manslaughter

All homicide offences have a common *actus reus* so the distinction between murder and the two forms of manslaughter lies in (a) the availability of partial defences (voluntary manslaughter) and (b) the presence or absence of *mens rea* (involuntary manslaughter). This flow chart captures the murder/manslaughter relationship.

Figure 6.3

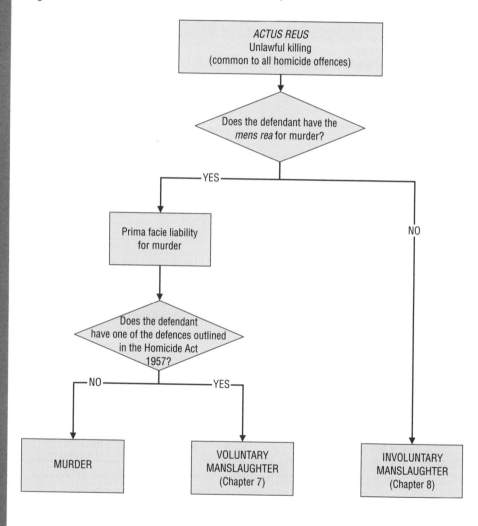

Chapter summary:
Putting it all together

☐ Can you tick all the points from the revision checklist at the beginning of this chapter?

☐ Take the **end-of-chapter quiz** on the companion website.

☐ Test your knowledge of the cases with the **revision flashcards** on the website.

☐ Attempt the problem question from the beginning of the chapter using the guidelines below.

☐ Go to the companion website to try out other questions.

Answer guidelines

See the problem question at the start of the chapter. A diagram illustrating how to structure your answer is available on the website.

Points to remember when answering this question

■ The question requires a focus of murder so no discussion of manslaughter or arson is needed.

■ Clarify the facts before attempting the question. For example, Doreen started the fire which burned Adam (fireman) and he killed himself. Issues: break in the chain of causation (suicide); oblique intention (primary aim was not causing death).

■ Work through the elements of murder methodically: *actus reus* then *mens rea*.

■ Do not allow instinctive reactions to get in the way of legal reasoning. You may sympathise with Deborah but that is irrelevant to whether she is liable for murder. Arguments based upon emotional notions of fairness attract little (or no) credit from examiners.

Make your answer really stand out

■ Do simple things well. Students often jump straight to the central issues without providing a basic framework for discussion. For example, although the issue of Adam's suicide as an intervening act requires discussion, this should follow from an outline of the elements of murder. Failure to define the offence and set out the *actus reus* and *mens rea* is a major weakness that is easily avoided by the use of a methodical problem-solving strategy.

■ Present a balanced argument making effective use of the facts. There are two sides to be presented (prosecution and defence) so be sure to consider both perspectives. A balanced answer attracts higher marks.

7
Voluntary manslaughter

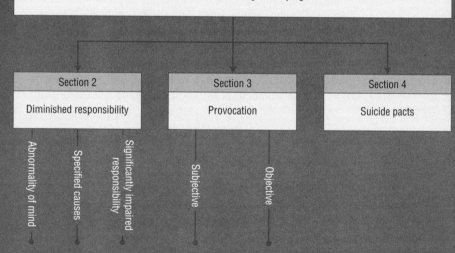

MURDER

Actus reus: unlawful killing
Mens rea: intention to kill or cause GBH
Mandatory sentence of life imprisonment

but

HOMICIDE ACT 1957

Provides three defences that reduce liability from murder to voluntary manslaughter which confers discretion in sentencing on the judge

Section 2	Section 3	Section 4
Diminished responsibility	Provocation	Suicide pacts

Abnormality of mind

Specified causes

Significantly impaired responsibility

Subjective

Objective

Revision checklist

What you need to know:

☐ Relationship between murder and voluntary manslaughter
☐ Nature and operation of diminished responsibility
☐ Two-stage test for provocation
☐ Operation of the reasonable man test

Introduction:
Voluntary manslaughter

Not all killings that fall within the scope of murder are regarded as equally culpable yet the mandatory penalty of life imprisonment will apply to them all unless a partial defence is available.

The Homicide Act 1957 provides three defences that reduce liability to manslaughter, giving the sentencing judge discretion and reflecting the lower level of culpability attached to certain killings.

The operation of the defences includes a measure of discretion resulting in blurred lines between voluntary manslaughter and murder, which makes this an important revision topic. As you revise this topic, give some thought to whether the defences achieve their aim of filtering out the less-culpable killings.

This chapter focuses on diminished responsibility and provocation. Suicide pacts are omitted as these rarely feature on the syllabus and do not raise any contentious issues.

Essay question advice

Essays on voluntary manslaughter fall into three main categories:

1 murder/manslaughter relationship
2 interplay between provocation and diminished responsibility
3 narrowly-focused essays, e.g. the reasonable man in provocation or discretion in diminished responsibility.

Thorough preparation is the key to success.

Problem question advice

Voluntary manslaughter arises because the defendant has a defence to murder so it is essential that *prima facie* liability for murder is established prior to any discussion of voluntary manslaughter. Problem questions may involve both defences together so be sure to unravel the facts carefully in search of relevant facts.

Sample question

Could you answer this question? Below is a typical problem question that could arise on this topic. Guidelines on answering the question are included at the end of the chapter, whilst a sample essay question and guidance on tackling it can be found on the companion website.

Problem question

Victor has been verbally abusive to Delia for several years. Delia suffers from depression and recently attempted suicide. During an argument, Victor waved a knife at Delia saying 'cut your wrists again'. She runs out of the house and returns later to find Victor asleep in bed holding the knife. Delia grabs the knife and cuts Victor's throat.

Discuss Delia's liability.

■ Diminished responsibility

This defence recognises that it is less culpable to kill when the mind is disturbed than it is to act in the same way when the mind is operating normally.

KEY STATUTORY PROVISION

Homicide Act 1957, s.2(1)

A person... shall not be convicted of murder if he was suffering from such abnormality of mind (whether arising from a condition of arrested or retarded development of mind or any inherent causes or induced by disease or injury) as substantially impairs his mental responsibility for his acts and omissions in doing... the killing.

Abnormality of mind

This is the essence of diminished responsibility. Section 2(1) specifies the sources from which abnormality of mind must arise but does not otherwise elaborate on its meaning. Case law has addressed this issue.

R v. Byrne [1960] 3 All ER 1

Concerning: abnormality of mind

Facts

The defendant was a psychopath who strangled and mutilated the victim whilst suffering from uncontrollable perverted sexual desires. His conviction for murder was quashed as it was held that inability to control such impulses was within 'abnormality of mind'.

Legal principle

'Abnormality of mind' was defined as 'a state of mind so different from that of ordinary human beings that the reasonable man would term it abnormal'. This expanded diminished responsibility to include uncontrollable impulses or behaviour and inability to exercise rational judgement.

This approach asks the jury whether (in light of medical evidence) they feel that the defendant's mind is significantly different to an ordinary person's mind.

Specified causes

Section 2(1) specifies that the abnormality of mind must arise from:

▪ arrested or retarded development;
▪ any inherent cause; or be
▪ induced by disease or injury.

REVISION NOTE

As diminished responsibility deals with mental abnormality, you might like to compare its operation with the defence of insanity (Chapter 17).

Any abnormality of mind not arising from these causes cannot give rise to diminished responsibility (*King* [1965] 1 QB 443) but the causes have been subject to interpretation by the courts to include a range of situations:

▪ epilepsy: *Campbell* (1986) 84 Cr App R 255

- Asperger's syndrome: *Reynolds* [2005] All ER (D) 249
- battered woman's syndrome: *Hobson* [1997] Crim LR 759
- depression: *Ahluwalia* [1992] 4 All ER 889
- paranoid psychosis: *Sanderson* (1993) 98 Cr App R 325.

EXAM TIP

Any suggestion of illness, depression or lack of perception, understanding, judgement or control should give rise to consideration to diminished responsibility if the defendant has killed.

Problem area: diminished responsibility and intoxication

If a defendant suffers from an abnormality of mind but killed whilst under the influence of alcohol (or drugs) it can be difficult to determine the contribution of each factor towards his behaviour: did he kill because he was intoxicated or because of his mental state? The House of Lords in *Dietschmann* have recently tackled this dilemma.

The situation is more straightforward if the defendant is an alcoholic. If this has progressed to the stage that it has damaged his brain or he is unable to resist the urge to drink, this falls within diminished responsibility (abnormality of mind due to disease): *R v. Tandy* (1988) 87 Cr App R 45.

Bear this distinction in mind in problem questions involving mental abnormality and intoxicated defendants.

KEY CASE

R v. Dietschmann [2003] 1 AC 1209

Concerning: abnormality of mind, intoxication

Facts

The defendant killed whilst heavily intoxicated and suffering from an adjustment disorder (depressed grief reaction following bereavement) amounting to an abnormality of mind. The trial judge directed the jury that diminished responsibility was only available if the defendant would have killed even if he had not taken a drink. The House of Lords ruled this was a misdirection.

Legal principle

Section 2(1) does not require abnormality of mind to be the sole cause of the killing. Even if the defendant would not have killed had he been sober, the contribution of the alcohol did not necessarily prevent the abnormality of mind from substantially impairing his mental responsibility and giving rise to diminished responsibility.

This means that the effect of alcohol must be ignored and attention focused on whether the abnormality of mind, irrespective of intoxication, substantially impaired the defendant's responsibility.

Substantially impaired responsibility

This is a broad term that gives the jury wide discretion to make moral decisions about whether the defendant's conduct should be categorised as murder or manslaughter.

EXAM TIP

In a problem question, identify facts that are likely to make the jury sympathetic towards the defendant, tipping them towards a verdict of manslaughter, or factors that might make them inclined to view the killing as murder.

■ Provocation

Diminished responsibility focuses on the defendant's state of mind and thus is concerned with internal factors. Provocation looks at the external events leading to the killing. It is based upon the notion that killing in the heat-of-the-moment is less culpable than premeditated killing in cold blood.

EXAM TIP

Provocation is only a defence to murder. Problem questions often involve non-fatal injuries inflicted as a result of provocation and this tricks students into discussing provocation. This fundamental (but common) mistake will lose marks. Remember, provocation is contained in the Homicide Act 1957 so is only relevant to *homicide* offences!

KEY STATUTORY PROVISION

Homicide Act 1957, s.3(1)

Where... there is evidence... that the person charged was provoked (whether by things done or by things said or by both together) to lose his self-control, the question whether the provocation was enough to make a reasonable man do as he did shall be... determined by the jury.

This establishes a two-stage test (see Figure 7.1).

Figure 7.1

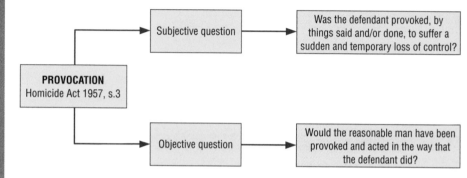

Things said and done

Provocation includes 'things done or things said or both together' (s.3) including:

- acts not intended to provoke, i.e. a baby crying (*Doughty* (1986) 83 Cr App R 319)
- acts not emanating from the defendant, i.e. acts of third parties or natural events (*Davies* [1975] 1 All ER 890).

Loss of control

Consider first the wholly subjective question of whether the defendant lost self-control. Without this, there is no possibility of provocation.

KEY CASE

R v. *Duffy* [1949] 1 All ER 932

Concerning: loss of self-control

Facts

The defendant killed her sleeping husband after a period of brutal treatment during which he refused to allow her to leave him.

Legal principle

The subjective requirement of provocation was defined as 'a sudden and temporary loss of self-control, rendering the accused so subject to passion as to make him or her for the moment not master of his mind'.

Problem area: provocation and lapse of time

The 'sudden and temporary' requirement precludes a defence if there is a lapse of time between provocation and killing. This was an issue in battered-women cases:

■ *Ahluwalia* [1992] 4 All ER 889: after years of violence, the defendant poured petrol over her sleeping husband who died in the ensuing fire.

The court would not accept a defence of provocation as the lapse in time was indicative of a 'cooling-off period' that was suggestive of a revenge attack. The possibility of 'slow-burn' reactions to violence was acknowledged but the court held that the greater the lapse in time between provocation and killing, the less likely it was that the requisite loss of control could be established. The appeal succeeded on the basis of diminished responsibility.

■ *Thornton* [1992] 1 All ER 306: the defendant's husband had been violent throughout their marriage. He threatened to kill the defendant and dared her to kill him first. She went into the kitchen, sharpened a knife and stabbed her husband in the stomach.

The court recognised the 'last straw' principle whereby a minor act can trigger loss of self-control if the defendant has endured years of abuse. It was held that, in cases involving cumulative provocation, the vital question was whether, at the moment that the fatal blow was delivered, the defendant was deprived of the self-control that she had previously been able to exercise.

It is important to consider what went on between the provocation and the killing and whether it is reasonable to characterise the defendant as 'out of control' notwithstanding any lapse of time.

EXAM TIP

In a problem question, try to isolate the following information:

■ What words/acts caused the loss of control?
■ How long after the provocation did the killing occur?
■ What did the defendant do during this gap in time?
■ Despite any lapse in time was there loss of control at the time of the killing?

The reasonable man

If loss of control is established, the second limb of provocation must also be satisfied for the defence to be established.

The reasonable man test established an objective standard of self-control against which the defendant's reaction is measured. It is not purely objective (the truly reasonable man would never lose control) as some characteristics of the defendant are attributed to the reasonable man.

There is consensus in case law that some characteristics of the accused should be given to the reasonable man but disagreement as to which characteristics this should include. There are two distinct schools of thought (see Figure 7.2).

Figure 7.2

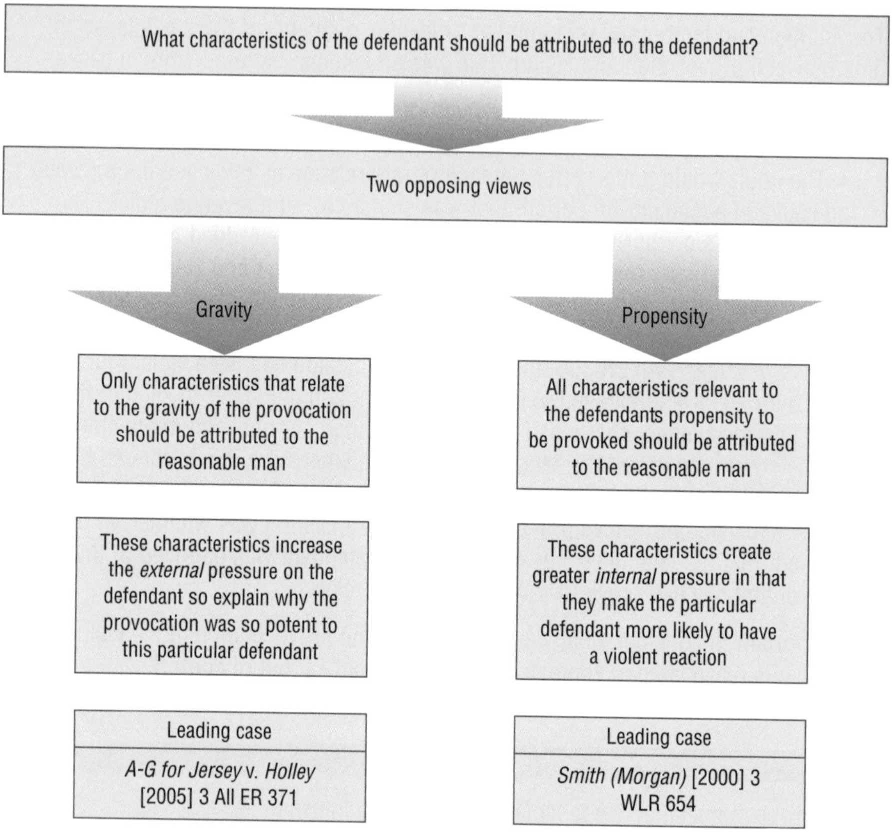

What characteristics of the defendant should be attributed to the defendant?

Two opposing views

Gravity

Only characteristics that relate to the gravity of the provocation should be attributed to the reasonable man

These characteristics increase the *external* pressure on the defendant so explain why the provocation was so potent to this particular defendant

Leading case

A-G for Jersey v. *Holley* [2005] 3 All ER 371

Propensity

All characteristics relevant to the defendants propensity to be provoked should be attributed to the reasonable man

These characteristics create greater *internal* pressure in that they make the particular defendant more likely to have a violent reaction

Leading case

Smith (Morgan) [2000] 3 WLR 654

KEY CASE

DPP v. *Camplin* [1978] 2 All ER 168

Concerning: reasonable man, attributed characteristics

Facts

The defendant, a 15-year-old boy, was buggered and then mocked about it. He lost control and hit out with a chapatti pan, killing his assailant. The trial judge directed the jury that the reasonable man was an adult, not a person of the defendant's age.

Legal principle

The House of Lords rejected this approach, stating that the reasonable man should have the same power of self-control as a person of the same age and sex as the defendant plus he should have the characteristics of the accused that affects the gravity of the provocation.

- The gravity approach was originally stated in *Camplin* as a measure to ensure the objective test operated fairly. Without relevant characteristics, the response of the accused to the provocation would seem disproportionate to the reasonable man, i.e. he would only understand the provocative impact of the victim's taunts if he had just been forcibly buggered.
- Following this, the reasonable man has the characteristics of the accused that relate to the provocation, even if this gives him inherently unreasonable characteristics: the reasonable glue-sniffer (*Morhall* [1996] AC 90).
- Problems arose with cases involving factors such as mental illness or alcoholism which did not affect the gravity of the provocation but which rendered the defendant more susceptible to loss of self-control. This led to a broadening of the law in *Smith (Morgan)* and the inception of the propensity approach to attributed characteristics.

KEY CASE

R v. *Smith (Morgan)* [2000] 3 WLR 654

Concerning: reasonable man, attributed characteristics

Facts

The defendant stabbed the victim during an argument. He claimed that depression had eroded his powers of self-control making him prone to violence. Under the traditional position, this could not be attributed to the reasonable man as it was not the subject of the provocation.

Legal principle

The House of Lords held that the reasonable man should be given whatever characteristics the jury felt were relevant to determine the reasonableness of the defendant's reaction. The majority rejected the approach that considered only characteristics relevant to the gravity of the provocation in favour of an approach which considered whether the defendant had exercised the level of self-control that could reasonably be expected of him in the circumstances.

This ruling was seen as settling the question of relevant characteristics but it was heavily criticised for virtually negating the objectivity of the test by attributing all the characteristics of the defendant to the reasonable man (making an objective test subjective). *Smith* (*Morgan*) was criticised in *Holley*.

Attorney-General for Jersey v. *Holley* [2005] 3 All ER 371

Concerning: reasonable man, attributed characteristics

Facts

The defendant was an alcoholic who killed his girlfriend with an axe whilst intoxicated. The Privy Council, by a majority of six to three, held that *Smith (Morgan)* was wrongly decided.

Legal principle

The Privy Council restated the requirement that only characteristics relevant to the *gravity* of the provocation could be attributed to the reasonable man. In determining the *standard* of self-control, the only relevant characteristics were age and sex.

- This resurrected the pre-*Smith (Morgan)* position but created confusion; the Privy Council stated that *Smith (Morgan)* was wrong yet it remained good law in England and Wales as Privy Council decisions are persuasive only.
- The Court of Appeal in *Mohammed* [2005] EWCA 1880 was faced with a dilemma over which line of authority to apply but followed *Holley* despite the status of the House of Lords decision in *Smith (Morgan)*. It was held that the 'narrow and strict test of a man with ordinary powers of self-control' was preferable to the 'excusability test' propounded in *Smith (Morgan)*.
- Make sure you understand the distinction between the two approaches. Which approach do you consider to be preferable?

FURTHER THINKING

Contentious current issues often crop up as essay topics. An answer should provide a clear statement of the central legal issue(s) and outline principles from leading cases. Gain additional credit by engaging in critical analysis of the cases, remembering to present both sides of the argument:

- As a defence that exists as a concession to human frailty, is it acceptable that such a narrow and exclusionary approach is taken to the characteristics attributable to the reasonable man (this is the argument against the *Camplin, Holley* position)?
- Does an approach that takes into account all characteristics of the accused dilute the test so that any claim of objectivity is meaningless (a criticism of the *Smith (Morgan)* position)?

Reading a case comment on the new developments will help to prepare you for an essay question: Elliot, C., 'Provocation: Objective Test' (2006) 70(1) *Journal of Criminal Law* 23.

Chapter summary:
Putting it all together

☐ Can you tick all the points from the revision checklist at the beginning of this chapter?

☐ Take the **end-of-chapter quiz** on the companion website.

☐ Test your knowledge of the cases with the **revision flashcards** on the website.

☐ Attempt the problem question from the beginning of the chapter using the guidelines below.

☐ Go to the companion website to try out other questions.

Answer guidelines

See the problem question at the start of the chapter. A diagram illustrating how to structure your answer is available on the website.

Points to remember when answering this question

■ Liability for voluntary manslaughter can only be established if the defendant has the *actus reus* and *mens rea* of murder so this should be the starting point of the answer.

■ Delia suffers depression so consider diminished responsibility as a possible defence.

■ Victor's taunts may constitute provocation so apply the two-stage test, taking particular care to consider the impact of the lapse in time between provocation and attack.

■ If both diminished responsibility and provocation seem to be established, include an evaluation of which defence seems stronger (and more likely to succeed) in your conclusion and explain why this is so.

Make your answer really stand out

■ As there is some doubt as to the correct test to apply in relation to the characteristics of the reasonable man, it would be appropriate to refer to both tests (*Smith* (*Morgan*) and *Holley*) and comment upon any difference that this makes to the outcome.

■ Explore alternative interpretations of the facts that present arguments both for and against liability: has Delia calmed down whilst she has been away or does her action in grabbing the knife indicate she is still in the grip of provocation? This adds balance and objectivity to your answer and is likely to attract extra credit from examiners.

8

Involuntary manslaughter

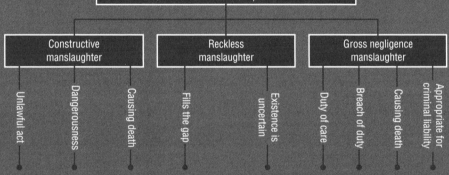

INVOLUNTARY MANSLAUGHTER

The defendant has the *actus reus* of murder (unlawful killing) but does not satisfy the *mens rea* of murder (intention to kill or cause GBH)

Constructive manslaughter
- Unlawful act
- Dangerousness
- Causing death

Reckless manslaughter
- Fills the gap
- Existence is uncertain

Gross negligence manslaughter
- Duty of care
- Breach of duty
- Causing death
- Appropriate for criminal liability

Revision checklist

What you need to know:

- [ ] Relationship between murder and involuntary manslaughter
- [ ] Distinction between voluntary and involuntary manslaughter
- [ ] Elements of constructive manslaughter
- [ ] Operation of gross negligence manslaughter
- [ ] Weaknesses in the law and proposals for reform

Introduction:
Involuntary manslaughter

Involuntary manslaughter covers situations in which the defendant has caused death but does not satisfy the *mens rea* requirements of murder; it is a less-culpable form of homicide.

This makes it a key revision topic as questions may test your ability to distinguish between levels of culpability in homicide offences, i.e. require an understanding of the relationship between murder and involuntary manslaughter.

There are two well-established categories of involuntary manslaughter (constructive and gross negligence) that largely require understanding of recognised legal principles whilst the existence of the third category – reckless manslaughter – is more controversial and requires a deeper grasp of policy issues. Awareness of the gaps in the law is essential as is an ability to comment upon proposals for reform.

Essay question advice

There are two main issues that can be explored in essay questions: (1) relationship between murder and involuntary manslaughter, and (2) interaction of the different types of involuntary manslaughter.

The second type of question should include discussion of the gap between constructive and gross negligence manslaughter so awareness of the potential of reckless manslaughter to fill this gap would be particularly valuable.

Either type of question requires a clear understanding of the function of each offence: ask, 'What type of conduct does this aim to penalise?'

Problem question advice

Problem questions involving death should start with a discussion of murder (the most serious homicide offence). Establish the common *actus reus* (unlawful killing) first and then move to consider the *mens rea* of murder. If it is not established, the next step is to consider involuntary manslaughter. Take care not to repeat points already discussed in relation to murder but refer back to that discussion when necessary; there is no credit to be gained from covering the same law twice in one answer.

Sample question

Could you answer this question? Below is a typical essay question that could arise on this topic. Guidelines on answering the question are included at the end of the chapter, whilst a sample problem question and guidance on tackling it can be found on the companion website.

Essay question

'Involuntary manslaughter is an offence of ill-defined boundaries covering the middle ground between murder and accidental death'. Critically evaluate the accuracy of this statement.

■ Constructive manslaughter

Constructive manslaughter (also known as unlawful dangerous act manslaughter) is a common law offence so its elements are found in case law. It builds (constructs) liability on some other (non-homicide) offence that has caused the victim's death and has three elements:

- Was the defendant's act unlawful?
- Was the unlawful act dangerous?
- Did the unlawful and dangerous act cause death?

Unlawful act

Constructive manslaughter requires an unlawful act. This must be a complete criminal offence: the *actus reus* and *mens rea* of an offence must be established. Civil liability will not suffice.

R v. *Lamb* [1967] 2 QB 981

Concerning: constructive manslaughter, unlawful act

Facts

The defendant pointed a gun at his friend as a joke. He knew that it contained bullets but that these were not in the 'fire' position. He pulled the trigger as a joke. The mechanism of the gun rotated the chamber so that the gun fired. The victim died of injuries sustained. The defendant's conviction for involuntary manslaughter was quashed on the basis that the defendant's actions did not amount to a criminal offence, not even common assault.

Legal principle

Involuntary manslaughter requires a criminally unlawful act. In the absence of the *actus reus* and *mens rea* of common assault being established, there was no unlawful act upon which liability for involuntary manslaughter could be constructed.

EXAM TIP

The requirement of a criminal offence as the basis of constructive manslaughter means that the starting point for any discussion of liability is to identify the *actus reus* and *mens rea* of an appropriate offence.

When looking for an offence upon which to base liability, there are a few important points to bear in mind as follows.

Act not omission

Constructive manslaughter can only be based on a positive act. Even if the defendant fails to act when he has a duty to do so (Chapter 2) and this causes death, there can be no liability for constructive manslaughter.

R v. *Lowe* [1973] QB 702

Concerning: constructive manslaughter, unlawful act

Facts

The defendant failed to call a doctor to attend to his ailing nine-week-old baby and she died soon after. His conviction for manslaughter was quashed.

Legal principle

Constructive manslaughter requires a positive act. An omission, even a deliberate omission, will not suffice.

Variable *mens rea*

The *mens rea* of constructive manslaughter corresponds with the *mens rea* of the unlawful act upon which liability is based. This means that it differs from case to case:

- Dan throws a brick through the window of a moving train, killing the driver. The basis of liability is criminal damage; the *mens rea* is intention or recklessness as to the damage/destruction of another's property.
- Dave slaps Victoria around the face during an argument. She falls, hits her head on the kerb and dies as a result. Liability is based upon battery; the *mens rea* is intention to apply unlawful force to the body of another (or recklessness thereto).

These examples illustrate the variability of the *mens rea* requirement. They also demonstrate the way that liability for constructive manslaughter is based upon some other offence, even if death is an entirely unforeseeable consequence.

EXAM TIP

If death arises from an attack, base liability on battery; this is the most straightforward non-fatal offence. Constructive manslaughter can be based upon any unlawful act, however trivial, so do not complicate matters by trying to establish one of the more serious offences. Never base liability on OAPA, s.18 (Chapter 10). If the ulterior intent for this offence exists (intention to cause GBH) and the victim has died, the appropriate offence is murder not involuntary manslaughter.

Dangerousness

The unlawful act must also be dangerous. The test of dangerousness in constructive manslaughter is outlined in *Church*.

KEY CASE

R v. *Church* [1966] 1 QB 59

Concerning: dangerousness

Facts

The defendant knocked the victim unconscious. Believing her to be dead, he pushed her body in the river where she drowned.

Legal principle

It is not enough that an unlawful act caused death. The unlawful act must be one that 'all sober and reasonable people would inevitably recognise must subject the other person to... the risk of some (albeit not serious) harm'.

In *Newbury and Jones*, the court considered whether the defendant must realise that his act is dangerous.

KEY CASE

R v. *Newbury and Jones* [1977] AC 500

Concerning: constructive manslaughter, dangerousness

Facts

The defendants threw a slab from a bridge onto a train, killing the guard. They appealed against their convictions for manslaughter on the basis that they did not appreciate that their conduct carried a risk of harm.

Legal principle

Provided that the defendant intentionally does an act which is both unlawful and dangerous, he need not recognise its dangerousness; there is no requirement that the defendant foresees a risk of harm to others arising from his unlawful act.

EXAM TIP

Look out for an unlawful act that a sober and reasonable person would realise carried a risk of harm to others even if the defendant is oblivious to the risk. Remember, in *Attorney-General's Reference (No 3 of 1994)* [1997] 3 WLR 421, Lord Hope stated 'dangerousness in this context is not a high standard. All it requires is an act likely to injure the other person'.

Causation

The unlawful and dangerous act must satisfy the ordinary rules of causation (Chapter 2); it must be both a factual and legal cause of death.

■ Gross negligence manslaughter

This is based not on criminal wrongdoing but on negligence, a concept usually associated with civil law. The offence is established if the defendant has been so negligent that criminal liability is appropriate. Note below:

■ Does the defendant have a duty towards the victim?
■ Is the defendant in breach of duty?
■ Did the breach of duty cause death?
■ Should the conduct be characterised as criminal?

Duty of care

The first step in establishing liability for gross negligence manslaughter is to identify a duty that exists between the defendant and the victim. There are two ways that this can arise:

- *Duty of care*: based on 'ordinary principles' of negligence (*Adomako*). Established readily in relation to professional and contractual relationships and in relation to road users.
- *Duty to act*: a person is only liable for failure to act if he has a duty to do so (Chapter 2).

Breach of duty

Breach of duty differs depending upon whether the defendant had a duty of care or duty to act:

- A *duty of care* is breached by poor performance of the duty. Evaluate what the defendant did and whether this fell short of what was expected of him (*Adomako*).
- A *duty to act* is breached by failure to act. Establish that the defendant has a duty to act and that he failed to do so.

KEY CASE

R v. Adomako [1995] 1 AC 171

Concerning: breach of duty

Facts

The defendant, an anaesthetist, failed to notice the patient's oxygen supply had become disconnected during an operation. The patient died from lack of oxygen.

Legal principle

The defendant's conduct must have 'departed from the proper standard of care incumbent upon him'. Where a person holds themselves out as possessing some special skill or knowledge then their conduct will be judged against the reasonably competent professional in the field.

EXAM TIP

When dealing with breach of duty, make a realistic argument about the expectations of *reasonably competent professionals* in the relevant field on the basis of the facts provided. You will not be expected to comment with authority on the standards and practices of doctors, for example, only to draw attention to facts which suggest that the defendant has fallen below a reasonable standard of competence.

Causing death

The ordinary principles of causation apply (Chapter 2); the defendant's breach of duty must be the factual and legal cause of death. Note that this may differ from the way in which causation is established in relation to murder:

Murder	Gross negligence manslaughter
Dave is a qualified gas fitter employed to service Vanessa's boiler. He rushes the job and reconnects the circuits incorrectly. This causes pressure in the boiler and it explodes during the night. Vanessa is killed in the ensuing fire.	
Vanessa would not have died 'but for' Dave's failure to wire the circuits correctly (factual causation). There are no other causes of her death so legal causation is established. Dave has caused Vanessa's death, satisfying the *actus reus* of murder (although probably not the *mens rea*).	As a qualified gas fitter contracted to service the boiler, Dave owes a duty of care to Vanessa. By failing to wire the boiler correctly, he has not performed his duties to the standard expected of a reasonably competent gas fitter thus is in breach of duty of care. As this breach has caused the explosion of the boiler which started the fire in which Vanessa died, Dave's breach of duty has caused Vanessa's death. (You could break this down into factual and legal causation if this had not been addressed earlier in the question.)
Establishing causation for the purposes of murder requires only that the defendant's conduct, taken as a whole, has caused death.	For the purposes of gross negligence manslaughter, the discussion of causation needs to be more specific and phrased in terms of duty and breach of duty.

EXAM TIP

The illustration above in relation to causation may seem like an insignificant point but it is just the sort of detail that demonstrates a comprehensive awareness of the requirements of the two offences and, as such, will really help your answer to stand out and impress the examiners.

Appropriate for the imposition of criminal liability

It is this fourth element that distinguishes civil negligence for causing death and gross negligence manslaughter. If the three preceding stages are satisfied, the defendant will still not attract criminal liability unless his conduct is 'so bad' that this is appropriate. This is a question of fact for the jury and it can take any factors into account in reaching a decision.

EXAM TIP

Make effective use of the facts in addressing this fourth element. What facts do you think would attract the sympathy of the jury (making it less likely to impose criminal liability) and what would make it inclined to convict.

Students often work through the first three stages then fail to apply the facts in relation to the fourth so careful attention to this stage could attract a lot of credit.

Reckless manslaughter

Constructive and gross negligence manslaughter may not cover all culpable killings. Constructive manslaughter requires the *actus reus* and *mens rea* of an offence and gross negligence manslaughter requires breach of a duty of care. If neither exists, the killing cannot fall within these categories of manslaughter.

This gap in the law could be filled by a third category of involuntary manslaughter based upon subjective recklessness although there is some academic debate about whether this offence exists.

FURTHER THINKING

The cases that have raised the possibility of the existence of reckless manslaughter and the problems that this would create for the law of involuntary manslaughter can be found in Elliot, C. 'What Direction for Gross Negligence Manslaughter?' (2001) 65(2) *Journal of Criminal Law* 145.

Reckless manslaughter would be established if the defendant has caused death with awareness that his conduct carried a risk of causing death or serious harm. It is based upon subjective recklessness so it must be established that the defendant was aware of a risk that his conduct could cause death or serious harm to another.

REVISION NOTE

Reckless manslaughter is based upon foresight of a risk of death or serious harm. In this respect, it is similar to oblique intention although that requires foresight of a risk that death/serious injury is a virtually certain consequence.

You might find it useful to revisit Chapter 3 to ensure that you can recognise the difference between oblique intention (giving rise to liability for murder) and subjective recklessness (the basis for involuntary manslaughter).

Chapter summary:
Putting it all together

☐ Can you tick all the points from the revision checklist at the beginning of this chapter?

☐ Take the **end-of-chapter quiz** on the companion website.

☐ Test your knowledge of the cases with the **revision flashcards** on the website.

☐ Attempt the essay question from the beginning of the chapter using the guidelines below.

☐ Go to the companion website to try out other questions.

Answer guidelines

See the essay question at the start of the chapter. A diagram illustrating how to structure your answer is available on the website.

Points to remember when answering this question

■ Set the context of the essay with a focused introduction. An explanation of the role of involuntary manslaughter in the structure of homicide offences would be useful here as a way of explaining how the offence occupies the 'middle ground' mentioned in the question.

■ Limit the level of descriptive detail. This question requires an explanation of constructive and gross negligence manslaughter but this should not be too lengthy. Practise writing concise summaries of the offences as part of the revision process.

■ Keep a focus on the question. In relation to each point included in your answer, ask yourself how it contributes to your argument about the 'ill-defined boundaries' of the offence. This will help you to avoid straying off-point.

■ Draw the strands of your answer together in an effective conclusion that goes to the heart of the issues posed in the question.

Make your answer really stand out

■ A better answer to this question will explain that the two established categories of involuntary manslaughter (a) overlap and (b) fail to cover all culpable killings and explain how reckless manslaughter could overcome these deficiencies.

■ Provide examples to support your argument. Is there any relevant case law or can you explain your point by reference to a hypothetical example? For example, can you think of a situation that falls within both constructive and gross negligence manslaughter, remembering that the first requires an unlawful dangerous act and the second a breach of duty of care?

■ Provide evidence of wider reading by incorporating references to articles and/or proposals for reform such as the Home Office (2000) report entitled *Reforming the Law on Involuntary Manslaughter*. This can be particularly useful when arguing that the current law is inadequate.

9
Assault and battery

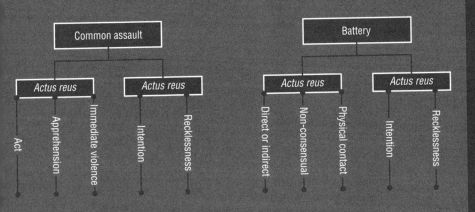

Revision checklist

What you need to know:

- [ ] The *actus reus* and *mens rea* of both offences
- [ ] The distinction between common assault and battery, and their relationship with OAPA, s.47
- [ ] The way in which the elements of the offences have been interpreted
- [ ] The operation of consent

Introduction:
Understanding common assault and battery

Common assault and battery are the least serious of the non-fatal offences.

This does not mean they are simple; in fact, they are amongst the more complex of the offences in terms of the interpretation of their elements. Therefore, this topic requires careful revision to master the complexities of the law.

Students tend to experience difficulties with these offences. This is largely because the terms 'assault' and 'battery' are in everyday use in a way that does not match their legal meaning. Remember to treat these offences as if you had no preconception of what they involve, learn their elements and apply them in a methodical way.

This chapter also deals with the defence of consent. You will find it here instead of with the other defences because it is a defence that only applies to these particular offences.

Essay question advice

Essays focusing exclusively on assault and/or battery are uncommon. You are more likely to encounter an essay that either:

(a) requires an analysis of these and other non-fatal offences as a broad category: this requires an understanding of how the offences relate to each other and the problems that arise from the overlap between them; or

(b) focuses on a narrow aspect of one of the non-fatal offences such as the elasticity of the immediacy requirement or the operation of consent as a defence.

New developments are fertile ground for essays so keep up-to-date with recent House of Lords decisions.

Assault and battery frequently arise with other non-fatal offences (Chapter 10) but can also combine with fatal, sexual or property offences as well as defences. This flexibility makes them popular with examiners but can create pitfalls for students who have been too selective in their revision.

If questions combine topics, ensure you are confident with them; marks are lost on partially answered questions.

Sample question

Could you answer this question? Below is a typical problem question that could arise on this topic. Guidelines on answering the question are included at the end of the chapter, whilst a sample essay question and guidance on tackling it can be found on the companion website.

Problem question

Danielle (13) asks David (14) to pierce her navel with a needle. She lies down and closes her eyes. David thinks that it will be difficult to get the needle through her navel so he pierces her ear instead. Danielle is furious as her parents have forbidden her to have her ears pierced. She chases David out of the house with an umbrella. Derek, Danielle's father, notices her pierced ear and beats her severely with a belt, causing bruising to her buttocks.

Discuss the liability of the parties.

∎ Distinguishing common assault and battery

Remember the following points to avoid common errors (see also Figure 9.1):

- Assault and battery are *two separate offences*. They are often referred to as a composite term as they frequently arise from the same incident.
- Common assault *never* involves physical contact.
- If there is physical contact, the defendant has committed a battery.

Figure 9.1

Timing of events →	
COMMON ASSAULT	**BATTERY**

Definition	
The defendant causes the victim to apprehend immediate unlawful violence	The defendant applies non-consensual physical contact to the victims body

In other words	
The victim sees that an attack is imminent	The attack on the victim takes place

For example	
Vincent sees Derek running towards him with an axe	Derek hits Vincent over the head with the axe

Common assault

KEY DEFINITION

Common assault is 'an act by which a person intentionally or recklessly causes another to apprehend immediate and unlawful personal violence (Law Commission (1993) *Legislating the Criminal Code*).

Three *actus reus* elements	Two *alternative mens rea* elements
an act	intention to cause apprehension of immediate violence
apprehension	
immediate violence	*or*
	subjective recklessness as to whether such apprehension is caused

Actus reus elements

The act

Assault requires a positive act so cannot be committed by omission (Chapter 2). There are no longer any limitations to the sort of act that will suffice.

KEY CASE

R v. *Ireland* [1998] AC 147

Concerning: assault by words/silence

Facts

The defendant made a series of silent calls causing the receipients to suffer anxiety, depression and stress. The House of Lords addressed the following issues:

- the nature of the act requirement in common assault
- whether 'bodily harm' included psychiatric injury (Chapter 10).

Legal principle

Words as an assault The House of Lords dismissed the long-standing principle that words could not amount to assault as 'unrealistic and indefensible', stating 'a thing said is a thing done'.

Silence as an assault Silent calls could be characterised as an omission (failure to speak) which would not provide a basis for assault. However, the House of Lords held that the silent calls were a positive means of communicating; the defendant intended his silence to communicate a threat thus constituting a positive act.

EXAM TIP

Problem questions frequently involve words as an assault so *Ireland* is an important case. Remember that the other requirements of the offence must also be satisfied.

A trickier situation involves silence: the defendant does not reply when asked, 'You're not going to hurt me, are you?' Remember, that *Ireland* distinguishes silent telephone calls (a positive form of communicating) and silence in person (which *may* still constitute an omission and thus cannot be the basis of assault).

Apprehension

The act must cause apprehension of violence. Apprehension, in this sense, does not mean fear; it means expectation. It is a common mistake (made by lecturers and judges as well as students) to use 'apprehension' and 'fear' interchangeably (see Figure 9.2).

Figure 9.2

FEAR	APPREHENSION
Darren drives past Vernon and shouts abuse and threats at him. Vernon is afraid as he knows Darren has a reputation for violence.	Vernon shouts abuse as Darren drives past. Darren is so angry that he stops the car and runs towards Vernon, waving his fists. Vernon is eager for a fight and races to confront Darren.
Vernon is fearful as he knows Darren is violent but he does not apprehend (anticipate) violence as Darren has driven away. Words can only constitute an assault if they cause an apprehension of immediate unlawful violence. Causing a general state of fearfulness will not suffice; there must be an expectation of an imminent attack.	Darren is waving his fists so Vernon is expecting violence to be imminent. He is not afraid; he is eager to fight. This will nonetheless amount to common assault as Vernon apprehends (anticipates) violence from Darren. The fact that he is not afraid is irrelevant.

EXAM TIP

■ A person may apprehend violence without being fearful (common assault).
■ A person may fear violence without expecting it is imminent (no offence).

Immediate violence

The immediacy requirement of common assault is consistent with the overall purpose of the offence which is to prohibit causing an expectation of imminent attack.

> **KEY CASE**
>
> ***R* v. *Ireland* [1998] AC 147**
>
> **Concerning: common assault, immediacy**
>
> **Facts**
>
> See page 101.
>
> **Legal principle**
>
> The House of Lords confirmed that only apprehension of *immediate* violence would suffice for assault. This was satisfied in relation to silent calls: 'What, if not the possibility of imminent personal violence, was the victim terrified about?'

R v. *Constanza* [1997] 2 Cr App R 492

Facts

As part of a stalking campaign, the defendant sent over 800 letters to the victim within eight months. The final letter was hand-delivered, giving rise to a charge of assault.

Legal principle

The Court of Appeal addressed the immediacy requirement by holding that the letter caused an apprehension of violence at *some time not excluding the immediate future*.

EXAM TIP

There is a distinction between:

▌ apprehension of immediate violence (common assault), and
▌ immediate apprehension of deferred violence (no offence).

Mens rea of assault

The three elements of the *actus reus* can be complicated but the *mens rea* of assault is reassuringly straightforward, requiring either:

▌ intention to cause apprehension of immediate unlawful violence (deliberately causing the *actus reus*); or
▌ subjective recklessness thereto (the defendant must foresee a risk that the victim will apprehend immediate unlawful violence).

REVISION NOTE

Revisit Chapter 3 to refresh your memory on subjective *Cunningham* recklessness. Remember it is based upon what the defendant actually foresaw rather than what he ought to have foreseen.

▌Battery

KEY DEFINITION

Battery is an act by which a person intentionally or recklessly inflicts unlawful personal violence on another (Law Commission (1993) *Legislating the Criminal Code*).

Three *actus reus* elements	Two *alternative mens rea* elements
direct or indirect	intention to make direct/indirect non-consensual physical contact with another
non-consensual	
physical contact	*or*
	subjective recklessness thereto

Actus reus elements

Direct or indirect

Battery is based upon physical contact, whether direct (one person touching another) or indirect (as in *Haystead* [2000] Crim LR 758 where the defendant hit a woman causing her to drop the baby she was holding. He was convicted of battery on the baby even though he did not touch it).

Non-consensual

Battery requires non-consensual touching. Consent may either be express (the victim agrees to contact) or implied (from the inevitable contact arising from participation in everyday life). Examples of implied consent were given in *Collins* v. *Wilcox* [1984] 3 All ER 374 as:

- jostling on the underground
- having one's hand seized in friendship
- amicable back-slapping.

Physical contact

There must be some physical contact with the victim. Even minor contact will suffice and it includes touching a person's clothing whilst they are wearing it (*Thomas* (1985) 81 Cr App R 331).

It is misleading to describe battery as 'violence' as it includes very minor physical contact and often results in no injury or very minor injuries. It is only the level of injury that distinguishes battery from OAPA, s.47 (Chapter 10) as demonstrated by the CPS Charging Standards for the two offences:

Battery	Actual bodily harm
Scratches/grazes	Temporary loss of sensory functions
Minor bruising	Extensive or multiple brusing
Superficial cuts	Minor cuts requiring stitching
Black eyes	Minor fractures

EXAM TIP

Focusing in the level of harm caused is a useful means of deciding what offence is appropriate in a problem question. The line between battery and s.47 is particularly important if consent is involved.

Mens rea of battery

As with common assault, the *mens rea* of battery is satisfied by *either* intention to make physical contact with the victim *or* by subjective recklessness as to such contact.

FURTHER THINKING

The issues raised by common assault and battery can seem complex particularly in relation to indirect violence. The following article provides a review of the case law and would be a useful read to deepen understanding in preparation for writing an essay on assault or battery: Hirst, M. (1999) 'Assault, Battery and Indirect Violence' *Criminal Law Review*, pp. 557–60.

Consent

All non-fatal offences require unlawful force. Consent can negate the unlawfulness of force. Why would someone consent to force? Remember that battery, for example, is not necessarily about punching and kicking but any physical contact; an unwanted hug is as much a battery as a slap around the face!

Problem area: scope of consent

The law on non-fatal offences strives for balance between *personal autonomy* (the right of individuals to control what happens to them) and *prevention of harm* (to individuals and society). Limitations on the availability of consent reflect policy considerations. The courts have addressed two questions:

- Where should the line be drawn between offences to which individuals should be able to consent freely and those where consent is not generally permitted?
- In relation to offences where consent is not generally permitted, what exceptions exist where consent should be recognised?

R v. Brown [1994] 1 AC 212

Concerning: consent, bodily harm

Facts

The defendants were sado-masochistic homosexuals charged with battery and offences under OAPA, ss.47 and 20 as a result of injuries caused during consensual sexual activity. They argued that the victims had consented to the activities and to the infliction of injuries.

Legal principle

The House of Lords ruled that consent was only a defence to conduct that did not result in bodily harm (battery). In relation to offences resulting in bodily harm, there were a range of exceptions where consent was a defence, such as surgery and sports, but these were justified on the basis of public interest. The House of Lords refused to enlarge that category to include consensual sexual activities, stating that it was not in the public interest for people to cause each other bodily harm for no good reason.

Brown was criticised for its apparent basis in morality and evident distaste for the defendant's activities. The principle has been refined and clarified in subsequent case law as illustrated in Figure 9.3.

FURTHER THINKING

The House of Lords in *Brown* recognised a range of exceptions to the general rule that a person cannot consent to bodily harm. The table on the companion website elaborates on the scope of these exceptions.

This will prepare you for an essay on consent which requires an ability to state the general rules, outline the exceptions and critically evaluate the current law.

Figure 9.3

Brown [1994] 1 AC 212	*Wilson* [1997] QB 47
Consent was no defence to charges arising from injuries inflicted during sado-masochistic homosexual encounters. It is not in the public interest that people cause each other injury for no good reason.	Consent was available for a man who branded his initials on his wife's buttocks with a soldering iron. What happens between a husband and wife in the privacy of the matrimonial home should not concern the criminal law.

CONFLICT?

Do these decisions give special status to marital relationships or do they reflect a distaste for homosexual activities.

The issue was resolved in a case involving sado-masochistic activity between a heterosexual cohabiting couple.

Emmett (1999) The Times, October 15

The defendant was not permitted to raise a defence of consent in relation to injuries inflicted during the course of consensual sado-masochistic activities with his heterosexual partner. The Court of Appeal held that it is not in the public interest for individuals to inflict harm on each other for the purposes of sexual gratification.

CONFLICT RESOLVED

Brown was followed in *Emmett*. Both cases involved the infliction of injury for the purposes of sexual pleasure, something that the law would not accept as justified in the public interest.	*Wilson* was distinguished in *Emmett*. Irrespective of the location of the branding, it was done for the purposes of adornment thus was analogous to a tattoo. Neither party derived sexual gratification from the imposition of the injury.

Chapter summary:
Putting it all together

☐ Can you tick all the points from the revision checklist at the beginning of this chapter?

☐ Take the **end-of-chapter quiz** on the companion website.

☐ Test your knowledge of the cases with the **revision flashcards** on the website.

☐ Attempt the problem question from the beginning of the chapter using the guidelines below.

☐ Go to the companion website to try out other questions.

Answer guidelines

See the problem question at the start of the chapter. A diagram illustrating how to structure your answer is available on the website.

Points to remember when answering this question

■ Make sure that you discuss all the parties. Work out who has done what as part of the planning process: Danielle (chasing David), David (piercing Danielle's ear), Derek (beating Danielle).

■ It would be a good idea to start with David here. He has committed the most serious offence (likely to be one of the OAPA offences covered in Chapter 10 rather than battery) and there is an issue of consent which can be built upon when discussing Derek's liability (in relation to lawful chastisement).

■ If you are given information in a problem question about the age of the parties or their relationship with each other, consider why this is included: does it have any implications about the liability of the parties? Here, for example, it is important to know that Derek is Danielle's father because of the possibility of reliance on lawful chastisement.

Make your answer really stand out

■ Remember that it does not matter if you cannot reach a definite conclusion. Sometimes the facts do not allow this so you will have to present an 'if X then Y' conclusion. For example, if David ran out of the house because he thought that Danielle was about to attack him with the umbrella, this will satisfy the *actus reus* of assault but if he ran because he was late for his dinner and he viewed Danielle's actions with amusement then the *actus reus* is not established and she will not be liable for assault. An answer that deals with both sides of the argument wherever possible will gain credit from examiners.

■ Demonstrate a sound approach to problem-solving by working through the elements of the offences in a methodical way.

10
Statutory non-fatal offences

INCREASING SERIOUSNESS / DECREASING PREVALENCE

GBH with intent

OAPA 1861, s.18

AR – wounding or
causing GBH
MR – intention/recklessness
plus ulterior intent

Wounding/inflicting GBH

OAPA 1861, s.20

AR – wounding or inflicting GBH
MR – intention or recklessness as to some harm

Assault occasioning actual bodily harm

OAPA 1861, s.47

AR – common assault or battery resulting in actual bodily harm
MR – intention or subjective recklessness to the common assault or battery only

Revision checklist

What you need to know:

- [ ] The *actus reus* and *mens rea* of the three offences
- [ ] The relationship between s.47 and common assault/battery
- [ ] The meaning of 'bodily harm' (actual/grievous) and 'wounding'
- [ ] The issues surrounding the *mens rea* of the offences: 'half *mens rea*' (s.47), *Mowatt* gloss (s.20), ulterior intent (s.18).

Introduction:
Understanding non-fatal offences

The Offences Against the Person Act 1861 (OAPA) is a collection of more serious non-fatal offences that do not fit together very well.

This is because they originally came from a variety of other sources but were collected together in a single statute. The result is a fair degree of overlap between offences but also some gaps in the law. Accept that there is confusion in this area of law and that this is the combined result of (a) the way in which OAPA was enacted and (b) over 140 years of judicial interpretation.

Essay question advice

There are plenty of complexities associated with non-fatal offences which could give rise to an essay question. Broad questions require an ability to see the 'big picture' of non-fatal offences and comment on the relationship between the offences whilst narrower questions may require more in-depth knowledge of a particular issue such as psychiatric injury or, as a recent development, the transmission of the HIV virus.

Problem question advice

Non-fatal offences can combine with fatal, sexual or property offences and defences as well as involving multiple parties (accessories and inchoate offences). This flexibility makes them popular with examiners but can create pitfalls for students who have revised non-fatal offences only to find them combined with a less-familiar topic.

Sample question

Could you answer this question? Below is a typical essay question that could arise on this topic. Guidelines on answering the question are included at the end of the chapter, whilst a sample problem question and guidance on tackling it can be found on the companion website.

Essay question

Many criticisms have been levelled against the Offences Against the Person Act 1861. In particular, it is said that its key provisions overlap with each other and that they are inconsistent in their use of terminology.

Discuss.

■ Assault occasioning actual bodily harm

KEY STATUTORY PROVISION

Offences Against the Person Act 1861, s.47

Whosoever shall be convicted on indictment of any assault occasioning actual bodily harm shall be liable... to imprisonment for any term not exceeding five years.

Section 47 states the penalty rather than defining the offence. Elaboration on the elements of the offence can be found in case law.

Two *actus reus* elements	Two *alternative mens rea* elements
the *actus reus* of common assault	the *mens rea* of common assault
or	*or*
the *actus reus* of battery	the *mens rea* of battery
plus	
actual bodily harm	

Actus reus elements

Section 47 can be satisfied in two different ways:

1 assault resulting in actual bodily harm (ABH)
2 battery resulting in ABH.

The only difference between s.47 and assault/battery is the level of harm that occurs. For this reason, it is sometimes called 'aggravated assault'.

Problem area: terminology

Both the offences are called 'assault occasioning ABH'; there is no separate offence of battery occasioning ABH. This is because the word 'assault' in s.47 actually means 'common assault or battery'. This can be confusing so make sure that you take care to use terminology correctly.

REVISION NOTE

Chapter 9 outlines the requirements of assault and battery so you might like to be sure that you are familiar with this before revising s.47.

Actual bodily harm

The common law definition of ABH is vague. *Donovan* [1934] 2 KB 498 described it as harm that is 'more than merely transient or trifling'.

REVISION NOTE

Revisit Chapter 9 and look at the table that shows the distinction made by the CPS between battery and ABH (page 105). This demonstrates the sorts of injuries considered to be 'more than transient and trifling'.

Occasioning

The common assault or battery must *occasion* (cause) the injury. This is straightforward in relation to battery; injuries are caused by physical contact. Common assault leading to injury is harder to understand – 'sticks and stones may break my bones but names will never hurt me'. There are two ways that threatening words/conduct can cause injury:

1 injuries sustained whilst escaping
2 psychological injuries.

Escape cases The courts have held that the defendant retains responsibility for injuries sustained whilst escaping from threatened (common assault) or actual (battery) violence (see Figure 10.1).

Figure 10.1

COMMON ASSAULT
Lewis [1970] Crim LR 647 The victim locked herself in the bedroom. Her husband started to break down the door so she jumped out of the window to escape. His common assault (breaking down the door caused her to apprehend immediate unlawful violence) was held to be the cause of the injuries sustained in the fall.

BATTERY
Roberts (1971) 56 Cr App R 95 The victim was a passenger in a car driven by the defendant. He committed a battery by interfering with the victim's clothing. She jumped out of the moving vehicle to avoid his attentions. It was held that the defendant's battery caused the injuries sustained by the victim in the fall.

EXAM TIP

If the defendant is not the *direct* cause of the victim's injuries, look for injuries caused *indirectly* particularly following common assault. Even though the victim chose to escape, injuries will be attributed to the defendant unless the victim's conduct was 'so daft' as to be unforeseeable (*Roberts*) (see Chapter 2 for more detail on causation).

Psychiatric injury The expansion of the law on non-fatal offences to include psychiatric injury is a relatively recent development as the cases in Figure 10.2 demonstrate.

KEY CASE

R v. *Ireland*; *Burstow* [1998] AC 147

Concerning: psychiatric injury

Facts

- *Ireland*: see Chapter 9
- *Burstow*: a stalking case in which the defendants bombarded an acquaintance with unwanted attention for three years.

The issue in both cases was whether the depressive symptoms suffered by the victims could amount to 'bodily harm' as this had previously been limited to physical injuries.

Legal principle

The House of Lords agreed that the draftsman of the OAPA would not have contemplated the inclusion of psychiatric injury within 'bodily harm'. However, the statute was of the 'always speaking' kind that expanded to accommodate new developments such as greater understanding of the link between mind and body. Harm to a person's mind that amounts to a recognised medical condition falls within 'bodily harm'.

Figure 10.2

Miller [1954] 2 QB 282
Injury to the victim's state of mind 'for the time being' amounted to 'bodily harm'.

Chan Fook [1994] 2 All ER 552
Held that 'body' is not limited to flesh, skin and bones but includes organs, nervous system and brain. Mere emotions such as fear, distress and panic are excluded.

Ireland [1998] AC 147
House of Lords confirmed *Chan Fook* and held that psychological injury could amount to actual bodily harm but that psychological injury should be a matter of expert evidence.

Burstow [1998] AC 147
House of Lords held that a sufficiently serious psychological injury could amount to grievous bodily harm.

Morris [1998] 1 Cr App R 386
In relation to psychological injury, expert evidence must be given by a psychiatrist not a general practitioner.

EXAM TIP

In problem questions, look out for mentions of depression, anxiety or sleeplessness resulting from the defendant's conduct as this suggests psychiatric injury. Remember that the House of Lords held that this can amount to ABH (*Ireland*) or GBH (*Burstow*) depending on its severity.

FURTHER THINKING

Psychiatric injury has been a popular essay topic. A good answer would address the following:

■ the policy behind the expansion of the law to include psychiatric injury
■ the legal background including *Miller* and *Chan Fook* with more detailed understanding of *Ireland* and *Burstow*
■ how psychiatric injury fits within the OAPA and any resultant difficulties
■ different approaches to physical and psychiatric injuries: a particularly clever argument would be to note that physical ABH is satisfied by bruises whilst psychiatric ABH requires a recognised psychological illness.

Mens rea elements

There are two parts to the *actus reus* of s.47: (1) assault or battery, or (2) ABH. The *mens rea* relates only to the first of these. This means that the *mens rea* of s.47 is identical to the *mens rea* of either assault or battery (whichever caused the ABH). This is why it is called an offence of *half mens rea* (see Figure 10.3).

Figure 10.3

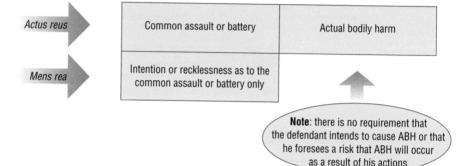

> **Note**: there is no requirement that the defendant intends to cause ABH or that he foresees a risk that ABH will occur as a result of his actions

---

KEY CASE

R v. *Savage* [1992] 1 AC 699

Concerning: half *mens rea*

Facts

The defendant poured her drink over the victim (battery). The glass slipped out of her hand, smashed and cut the victim. Her conviction under s.47 related to this injury. Her appeal against conviction was based on lack of *mens rea*: she argued that she neither intended injury nor foresaw that injury would be caused.

Legal principle

The House of Lords dismissed the appeal, holding that the *mens rea* of s.47 required intention or subjective recklessness in relation to the common assault or battery only. There was no requirement of intention or foresight in respect of the injury caused by the assault or battery.

The facts of *Savage* can be illustrated using the half *mens rea* diagram (Figure 10.4) with the facts inserted as shown:

Figure 10.4

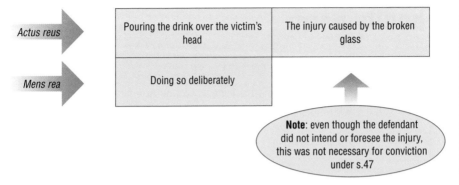

Actus reus

Pouring the drink over the victim's head	The injury caused by the broken glass

Mens rea

Doing so deliberately

Note: even though the defendant did not intend or foresee the injury, this was not necessary for conviction under s.47

Can you see how the principle of half *mens rea* allowed the defendant to be convicted when a full *mens rea* requirement would have led to acquittal?

Half *mens rea* makes it easier to establish liability for s.47. A defendant who has the *actus reus* and *mens rea* for a battery (or common assault) will be liable for the more serious offence under s.47 if the harm is greater than he planned or foresaw. This is justified because he has crossed the threshold into criminal behaviour by committing common assault/battery so will be liable for the consequences of his actions. The half *mens rea* principle is also a recognition that it is difficult to control the level of harm inflicted so a person who intends only battery cannot escape liability for a more serious offence if he inadvertently causes more serious harm.

You will find some excellent analysis of the impact of *Savage* (and the joined appeal in *Parmenter* which relates to the *mens rea* of s.20) in the following article that would be useful reading in preparation for an essay question: Stone, R., 'Reckless Assaults after *Savage* and *Parmenter* ' (1992) OJLS 578.

Use the flow charts on the companion website to develop a methodical approach to tackling problem questions on s.47.

Wounding or inflicting grievous bodily harm

KEY STATUTORY PROVISION

Offences Against the Person Act 1861, s.20

Whosoever shall unlawfully and maliciously wound or inflict any grievous bodily harm upon any other person, either with or without a weapon or instrument, shall be... liable to... five years' imprisonment.

Two *alternative actus reus* elements	Two *alternative mens rea* elements
wounding	intention
or	*or*
inflicting grievous bodily harm	recklessness as to the wound or the infliction of GBH

The combination of *actus reus* and *mens rea* elements give rise to four different ways that s.20 may be satisfied:

1 intentional wounding
2 intentional infliction of GBH
3 reckless wounding
4 reckless infliction of GBH.

Actus reus elements

Wounding and grievous bodily harm

KEY DEFINITIONS

GBH A general term meaning 'really serious harm': *DPP* v. *Smith* [1961] AC 290.

Wound A break in the continuity of both layers of the skin: *C* v. *Eisenhower* [1984] QB 331.

These two forms of *actus reus* cover a wide range of harm. They will often overlap, i.e. an injury will amount to both a wound and GBH, but this is not always the case: not all wounds are serious and not all serious injuries involve a break in the continuity of the skin.

Students tend to get confused on this point, often treating 'wound' and 'GBH' as interchangeable terms. The table below demonstrates the distinction between the terms:

Wound only	Wound and GBH	GBH only
Minor cut	Deep repeated cuts	
	broken bones piercing the skin	broken bones
		fractured skull
Syringe puncture		
		Psychiatric injury

Infliction

It was always thought that the requirement that GBH be *inflicted* on the victim meant something different to the requirement under s.18 that GBH was *caused* to the victim. However:

▪ in *Burstow*, it was held that there is no distinction between 'cause' and 'inflict' in relation to psychiatric injury
▪ in *Dica* [2004] QB 1257, it was held that this also applied in relation to physical harm (this concerned the infliction of GBH by transmission of HIV during intercourse).

These cases make it clear that the different terminology used in ss.20 and 18 is an unintended consequence of the amalgamation of offences from different sources into OAPA rather than a deliberate attempt to use different language to differentiate between inflicting and causing GBH.

Mens rea of s.20

Section 20 refers to *malicious* wounding or infliction of GBH. 'Maliciously' denotes two alternative *mens rea* states:

1 *intentional* wounding or infliction of GBH, or
2 *recklessly* wounding or inflicting GBH.

Section 20 is based upon *subjective* recklessness. However, case law has modified the traditional *Cunningham* test using the *Mowatt* gloss to create a particular form of subjective recklessness which applies only to OAPA, ss.20 and 18 (see Figure 10.5).

Figure 10.5

Pure *Cunningham* recklessness	Modified *Cunningham* recklessness
Requires that the defendant foresees a risk that his conduct will cause the prohibited consequence (*actus reus*). In relation to s.20, this would require that the defendant foresaw a risk that his conduct would wound or result in the infliction of GBH. Foresight of the risk of harm less than GBH would not suffice.	The *Mowatt* gloss on *Cunningham* recklessness catches defendants who foresee that their actions will cause some harm but who do not expect it to be so serious that it amounts to GBH. **The test of recklessness required for s.20 is therefore foresight of a risk of *some* harm, albeit not harm of the severity that actually occurred.**

KEY CASE

DPP v. *Parmenter* [1992] 1 AC 699

Concerning: recklessness, *Mowatt* gloss

Facts

The defendant's rough handling of his child caused broken bones. It was accepted that he had not intended to cause injury nor had he realised that there was a risk of injury. The trial judge directed the jury in terms of what the defendant *should have foreseen* would result from his actions.

Legal principle

The House of Lords upheld the ruling of the Court of Appeal that this was a misdirection.

- The standard of recklessness is *subjective* based upon what the defendant actually foresaw not what he ought to have foreseen.
- Foresight of the consequences was required but *not* foresight of their magnitude. This confirms the *Mowatt* gloss that foresight of *some* harm will suffice.

KEY STATUTORY PROVISION

Offences Against the Person Act 1861, s.18

Whosoever shall unlawfully and maliciously... wound or cause any grievous bodily harm... with intent... to do some grievous bodily harm to any person or with intent to resist or prevent the lawful apprehension or detainer of any person shall [be liable] to imprisonment for life.

■ Grievous bodily harm with intent

Two *alternative actus reus* elements	Two *cumulative mens rea* elements
wounding	maliciousness (regarding wound/GBH)
or	*and*
causing grievous bodily harm	ulterior intent (to cause GBH or resist/prevent lawful detention)

This combination of *actus reus* and *mens rea* requirements means that there are four different manifestations of s.18 (see Figure 10.6).

Figure 10.6

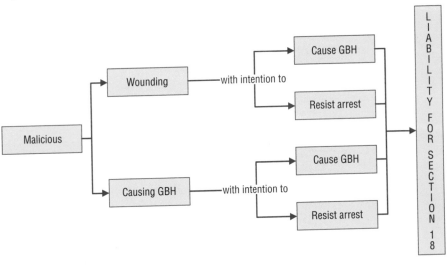

Actus reus elements

Wounding/causing GBH

There is little distinction remaining between 'cause' and 'inflict' thus the *actus reus* of s.18 is the same as s.20 *except* that s.18 covers GBH caused by omission. Section 20 requires that GBH is inflicted by a positive act.

EXAM TIP

Impress the examiner with this frequently overlooked point. There is credit to be gained by explaining (concisely) why a particular offence is not relevant:

For example: 'The defendant's failure to act caused serious injury to the victim. *As liability for s.20 cannot be based on omission*, the defendant may be liable under s.18'. This will gain greater credit than: 'The defendant has caused serious injury to the victim so may be liable under s.18.'

Mens rea elements

Section 18 has two *mens rea* requirements, both of which must be satisfied (see Figure 10.7).

Figure 10.7

STAGE 1 – MALICE
Was the wound or GBH caused intentionally or recklessly?
Remember that recklessness in this sense is subjective (as discussed in relation to s.20 above) so requires that the defendant was aware of the risk of some harm arising from his conduct.

STAGE 2 – ULTERIOR INTENT
Did the defendant possess ulterior intent?
Was he acting with the intention of: (a) causing GBH, or (b) resisting or preventing lawful arrest?

Malice

Intention or modified subjective recklessness as to causing of GBH or wound (as s.20).

Ulterior intent

This refers to the defendant's purpose in acting as he did.

- The defendant must intend to cause GBH rather than have a general intention to cause harm.
- An intention to wound will not suffice. Wounding only satisfied s.18 if it was caused with an intention to cause GBH or resist/prevent arrest.

- Intention to resist/prevent arrest covers the arrest of the defendant or a third party.
- There must be awareness of the arrest. A defendant who mistakenly thinks he (or another) is being attacked is not acting to resist/prevent arrest.
- The arrest must be lawful. Resisting an unlawful arrest is not sufficient to establish ulterior intent. However, resisting a lawful arrest in the mistaken belief that it is unlawful will satisfy the ulterior intent.

The requirements of ss.20 and 18 can cause confusion. The flow chart on the website should help you to work through problem questions in a methodical manner.

Chapter summary:
Putting it all together

TEST YOURSELF

☐ Can you tick all the points from the revision checklist at the beginning of this chapter?

☐ Take the **end-of-chapter quiz** on the companion website.

☐ Test your knowledge of the cases with the **revision flashcards** on the website.

☐ Attempt the essay question from the beginning of the chapter using the guidelines below.

☐ Go to the companion website to try out other questions.

Answer guidelines

See the essay question at the start of the chapter. A diagram illustrating how to structure your answer is available on the website.

Points to remember when answering this question

■ The criticisms mentioned in the question concern overlap between offences and inconsistent terminology. If you cannot address these points, you should not attempt this question even if you feel that there are other criticisms that you could make about the statute.

■ The question specifies OAPA so you should only include references to common assault and battery (Chapter 9) so far as these are relevant, i.e. in relation to s.47.

■ Work out a clear structure to your answer.

■ Questions inviting criticism give scope to comment on proposals for reform or at least question whether reform is needed.

Make your answer really stand out

The question refers to 'many criticisms' then goes on to specify two in particular. A good answer will pick up on the fact that this wording does not preclude discussion of the other criticisms so these should be included, preferably after the specified criticisms have been addressed.

11
Sexual offences

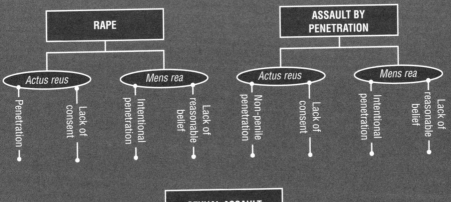

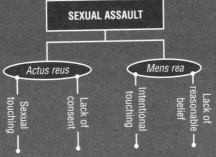

Revision checklist

What you need to know:

- [ ] *Actus reus* and *mens rea* of the offences
- [ ] Distinctions between the Sexual Offences Act 2003 and the previous law
- [ ] Role of consent, including operation of presumptions
- [ ] Relationship between the three offences

Introduction:
Understanding Sexual Offences

There was sweeping reform and modernisation of sexual offences in 2003.

This chapter focuses on three key offences: rape, assault by penetration and sexual assault. It is important, in the early days of new legislations, to be aware of the old law as a basis for comparison. Moreover, much of the old case law is still relevant to the interpretation of the new law so awareness of both is essential to success in this area.

Essay question advice

Recent legislative reform makes this a popular essay topic. An essay could focus on a particularly offence, i.e. rape, or ask more generally whether the new law is more effective. The scope of a general essay should be determined by reference to your course content so be sure that you are familiar with the sexual offences on your syllabus.

Problem question advice

Problem questions could cover a range of sexual offences, in which case a detailed knowledge of the range of offences and their relationship with each other is necessary, or could combine one of the sexual offences, often rape, with other offences. A combination of rape and fatal or non-fatal offences against the person is common but you should be aware of the possibility of rape arising with other, less usual, offences and, of course, defences; a defendant who has been raped may attack the rapist thus raising issues of self-defence, for example.

Sample question

Could you answer this question? Below is a typical problem question that could arise on this topic. Guidelines on answering the question are included at the end of the chapter, whilst a sample essay question and guidance on tackling it can be found on the companion website.

Problem question

Vanya (14) arrives at a party, drinks large quantities of gin and falls asleep. Richard tells Derek (14) (who has not been drinking) that Vanya wants to have intercourse with him and is waiting in the bedroom. Derek goes into the darkened room and sees Vanya lying on the bed. He touches her arm and she murmurs, 'Make love to me.' Derek engages in intercourse with Vanya, during which she shouts 'Richard' on several occasions. Derek is confused by this but does not stop.

Discuss Derek's liability for rape. How would your answer differ if these events occurred in 2002?

■Rape

Sexual Offences Act 2003, s.1(1)

A person (A) commits an offence if –

(a) he intentionally penetrates the vagina, anus or mouth of another person (B) with his penis,
(b) B does not consent to the penetration, and
(c) A does not reasonably believe that B consents.

Two *actus reus* elements	Two *mens rea* elements
Penile penetration by A of the vagina, anus or mouth of B	Intentional penetration
Absence of B's consent	A lacks a reasonable belief in B's consent

Compare the scope of the offence created by this definition with the old law (Figure 11.1).

Figure 11.1

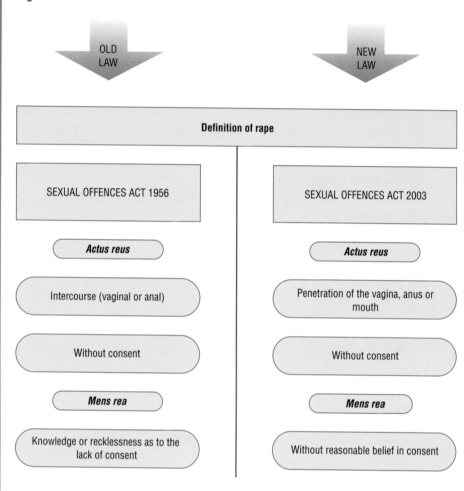

Penetration

The first aspect of the *actus reus* concerns the physical act. SOA 2003, s.79(2) defines penetration as 'continuing act from entry to withdrawal'.

This definition means that an initially lawful act becomes rape if consent is revoked during intercourse. This mirrors the position under the old law.

Consent

There are two roles for consent in the offence of rape. See Figure 11.2.

Figure 11.2

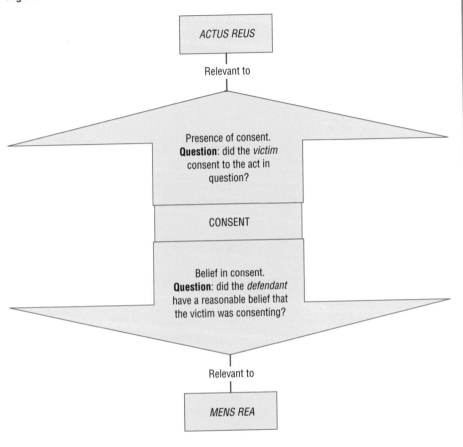

ACTUS REUS

Relevant to

Presence of consent.
Question: did the *victim* consent to the act in question?

CONSENT

Belief in consent.
Question: did the *defendant* have a reasonable belief that the victim was consenting?

Relevant to

MENS REA

EXAM TIP

There is a difference between (a) whether the victim actually consents to penetration (*actus reus*) and (b) whether the defendant believes that she or he consents to penetration (*mens rea*). A good answer will demonstrate an understanding of the difference between the two by identifying facts from the problem which relate to each aspect of consent.

Scrutinise the facts of the question for evidence of both consent and belief in consent: for example, Veronica struggles with Denis during intercourse (lack of consent: *actus reus*) which he takes as evidence of her enthusiasm (belief in consent: *mens rea*).

Absence of consent

Lack of consent is part of the *actus reus* of rape. The old law offered little guidance on the meaning of consent, leaving it to the jury to decide on the basis of 'good sense, experience and knowledge of human nature and modern behaviour': *Olugboja* [1982] QB 320. SOA 2003 provides greater guidance by creating three different approaches to consent (see Figure 11.3).

Figure 11.3

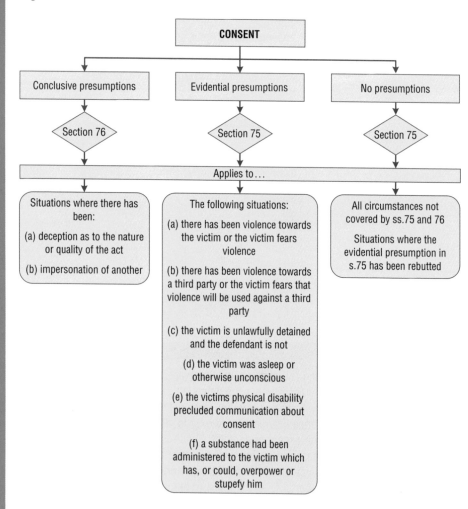

This is quite complicated. In relation to ss.75 and 76, the prosecution have to establish one of the listed circumstances rather than having to prove that there was no consent. The definition of consent is found in s.74. This must be applied when there are no conclusive or evidential presumptions and where the defendant rebuts the evidential presumption of consent.

KEY STATUTORY PROVISION

Sexual Offences Act 2003, s.74

A person consents if he agreed by choice, and has the freedom and capacity to make that choice.

EXAM TIP

There is no case law that interprets s.74 yet. It will be worth remembering that cases may come through as your course progresses so be sure to keep up-to-date with relevant developments. It would also be worth checking the companion website on a regular basis to see whether the law has changed.

Belief in consent

Under the previous law, a defendant could avoid liability for rape if he had an honestly-held mistaken belief in consent, even if that was unreasonable: *DPP* v. *Morgan* [1976] AC 182 (often called 'the rapist's charter).

The new position reverses this by introduction of a requirement that the defendant's belief in consent must be reasonable.

KEY STATUTORY PROVISION

Sexual Offences Act 2003, s.1(2)

Whether a belief is reasonable is to be determined having regard to all the circumstances including any steps A has taken to ascertain whether B consents.

Intention

The defendant's penetration of the vagina, anus or mouth must be intentional. This mirrors the requirement of intentional intercourse under the old law.

Figure 11.4

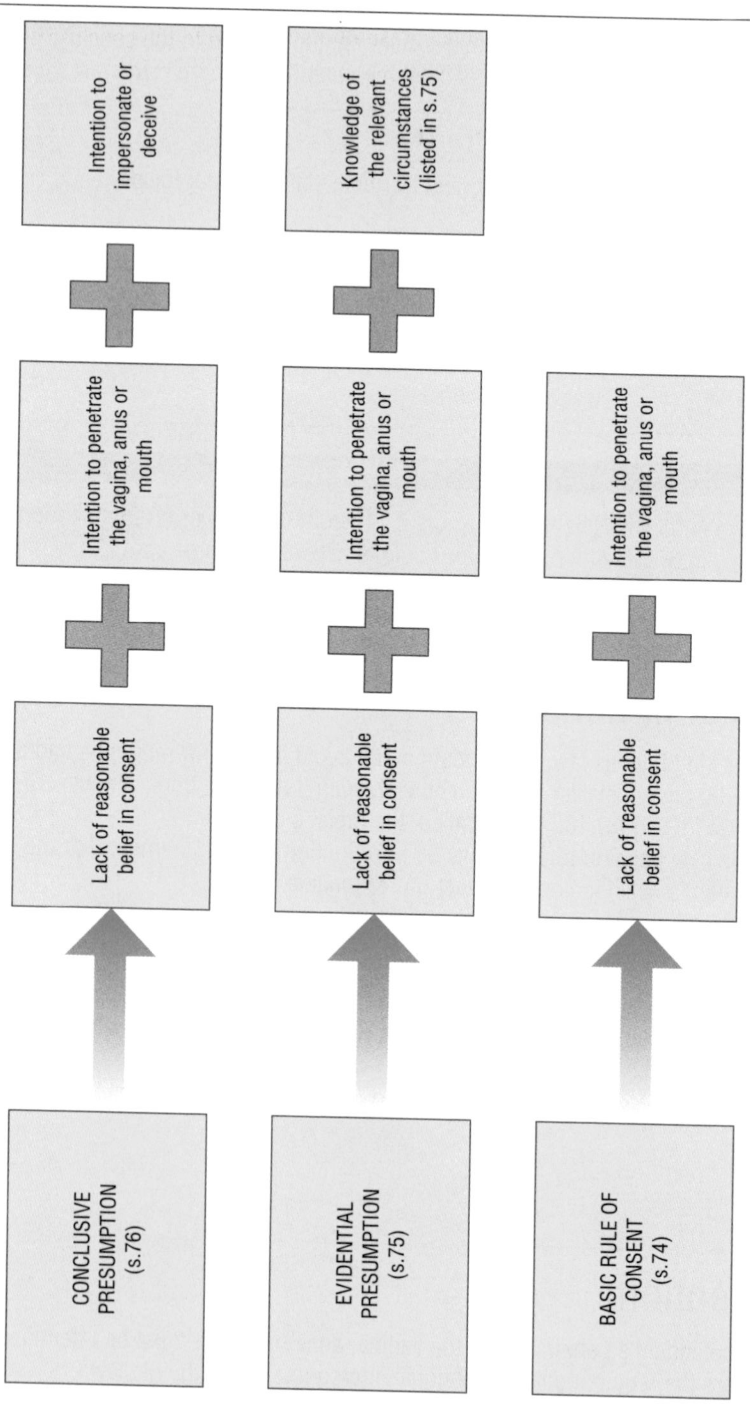
CONCLUSIVE PRESUMPTION (s.76)
Lack of reasonable belief in consent
Intention to penetrate the vagina, anus or mouth
Intention to impersonate or deceive
EVIDENTIAL PRESUMPTION (s.75)
Lack of reasonable belief in consent
Intention to penetrate the vagina, anus or mouth
Knowledge of the relevant circumstances (listed in s.75)
BASIC RULE OF CONSENT (s.74)
Lack of reasonable belief in consent
Intention to penetrate the vagina, anus or mouth

There is an additional *mens rea* requirement in relation to the conclusive and evidential presumptions; this creates three potential *mens rea* structures for rape (see Figure 11.4).

■ Assault by penetration

This is an important development in the law introduced to bridge the gap between rape and sexual assault (previously indecent assault). Prior to its introduction, all non-consensual sexual attacks short of rape were covered by a single offence thus giving little measure of relative seriousness. Assault by penetration elevates non-penile penetration to an equivalent seriousness with rape. See Figure 11.5.

Figure 11.5

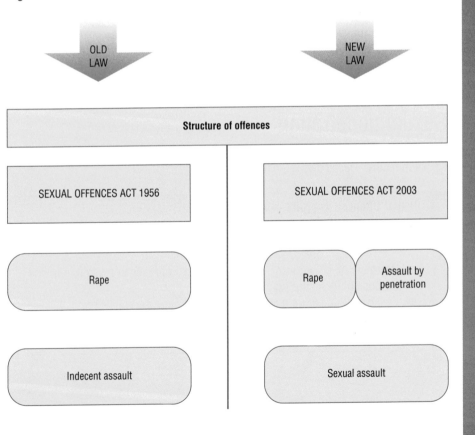

KEY STATUTORY PROVISION

Sexual Offences Act 2003, s.2(1)

A person (A) commits an offence if –

(a) he intentionally penetrates the vagina or anus of another person (B) with a part of his body or anything else,

(b) the penetration is sexual,

(c) B does not consent to the penetration, and

(d) A does not reasonably believe that B consents.

This replicates several features of rape but is limited to penetration of the vagina or anus. It can, however, by committed by a man or woman.

Two *actus reus* elements	Two *mens rea* elements
Non-penile sexual penetration of the vagina or anus	Intentional penetration
Absence of B's consent	A lacks a reasonable belief in B's consent

Sexual penetration

The only unexplored element concerns the requirement that the penetration must be sexual in nature. This is defined in s.78.

KEY STATUTORY PROVISION

Sexual Offences Act 2003, s.78

Penetration, touching or other activity is sexual if a reasonable person would consider that –

(a) Whatever its circumstances or any person's purpose in relation to it, it is because of its nature sexual or,

(b) Because of its nature it may be sexual and because of its circumstances or the purpose of any person in relation to it (or both) it is sexual.

There are complexities surrounding this approach to the definition of 'sexual'. The role of the assault by penetration also raises questions: does it put non-penile penetration on the same level of seriousness of rape (by separating it from other forms of sexual assault and creating a maximum penalty of life imprisonment) or does it give the message that non-penile penetration is less serious than rape (by separating the two offences and failing to give non-penile penetration the symbolic label of 'rape').

The following article considers these and other issues raised by the new legislation. There is a clear account of the new law and some thoughtful evaluation of its efficacy so it would be good preparation for an essay: Temkin, J. and Ashworth, A., 'Rape, Sexual Assaults and Consent' [2004] *Criminal Law Review* 328.

■ Sexual assault

This covers all non-penetrative sexual violation thus is an offence of immense scope.

<table>
<tr><td rowspan="7">KEY STATUTORY PROVISION</td></tr>
<tr><td>

Sexual Offences Act 2003, s.3(1)

A person (A) commits an offence if –

(a) he intentionally touches another person (B),
(b) the touching is sexual,
(c) B does not consent to the touching, and
(d) A does not reasonably believe that B consents.
</td></tr>
</table>

There is clear progression to the offences from non-consensual penile penetration (rape) to non-consensual non-penile penetration to the least serious offence involving non-consensual sexual touching. The consistency in language means that sexual assault breaks down into by-now familiar elements:

Two *actus reus* elements	Two *mens rea* elements
Sexual touching	Intentional touching
Absence of B's consent	A lacks a reasonable belief in B's consent

As the meaning of 'sexual' has been considered in relation to assault by penetration, the only unfamiliar element in this offence is that of 'touching'. The breadth of the definition demonstrates the reach of this offence.

KEY STATUTORY PROVISION

Sexual Offences Act 2003, s.79(8)

Touching includes touching –

(a) With any part of the body
(b) With anything else
(c) Through anything else.

This makes it clear that no touching is excluded, however brief or transient. Remember that this is qualified by the requirement that the touching is sexual.

Chapter summary:
Putting it all together

TEST YOURSELF

- [ ] Can you tick all the points from the revision checklist at the beginning of this chapter?
- [ ] Take the **end-of-chapter quiz** on the companion website.
- [ ] Test your knowledge of the cases with the **revision flashcards** on the website.
- [ ] Attempt the problem question from the beginning of the chapter using the guidelines below.
- [ ] Go to the companion website to try out other questions.

Answer guidelines

See the problem question at the start of the chapter. A diagram illustrating how to structure your answer is available on the website.

Points to remember when answering this question

■ The question requires an application of current and previous rape law. Make sure that you are able to deal with both before tackling such a question.

■ As there is one party (Derek) and one offence (rape), this should signal that a detailed consideration of the offence is needed. Questions involving multiple issues/parties invite a more superficial analysis.

■ Work through the elements of the current law in a methodical manner, establishing the *actus reus* before moving onto the *mens rea*. This is particularly important in relation to rape because consent plays a role in both elements of the offence.

■ Look out for any suggestion that the conclusive or evidential presumptions are raised.

Make your answer really stand out

■ The application of the evidential presumptions is complicated. Remember that if they are rebutted, consent falls to be determined under s.74.

■ Make effective use of the facts to argue both for and against liability. This will be particularly important in relation to consent, under both old and new law.

■ You should reach a conclusion that shows that conviction is far less likely under the old law thus there is scope for a thoughtful conclusion on the differences in the law and the efficacy of SOA 2003 that will really impress your examiner.

12
Criminal damage

CRIMINAL DAMAGE
Section 1(1) CDA 1971
AR: damage/destruction of property belonging to another
MR: intention or recklessness

AGGRAVATED CRIMINAL DAMAGE	ARSON
Section 1(2) CDA 1971	Section 1(3) CDA 1971
With intention to endanger life or being reckless whether life is endangered	Damage/destruction caused by fire

Revision checklist

What you need to know:

- [ ] *Actus reus* and *mens rea* of the offences
- [ ] The relationship between the basic and aggravated offences
- [ ] The scope of 'lawful excuse' and the role of 'consent' and 'protection of property'
- [ ] The test of recklessness and implications of *R* v. *G* [2004] 1 AC 1034

Introduction:
Understanding criminal damage

Criminal damage is a relatively straightforward offence involving damage or destruction of property.

The elements of the offence rarely cause problems for students but the 'defences' require more careful thought.

The basic offence is supplemented by two more serious variants: aggravated criminal damage and arson. These carry higher penalties due to the greater risk of harm to people: aggravated criminal damage involves volitional endangerment of life whilst the unpredictability of fire causes greater danger to life. Both offences have the basic offence at their core so can be regarded as criminal damage plus an additional element.

Essay question advice

Criminal damage essays are uncommon but recent developments in recklessness are a potential essay topic. This requires sound knowledge of the law pre- and post-*R* v. *G* and ability to comment on the implications for criminal damage. Other possible areas include the defences as these raise more complexity than the elements of the offence.

Problem question advice

Criminal damage is a popular problem topic. It is used to test knowledge of omissions (Chapter 2) and often appears as the 'unlawful act' in constructive manslaughter (Chapter 8).

The shift away from an objective test of recklessness is likely to give rise to problems that combine criminal damage with non-fatal offences (which use a different test of subjective recklessness: Chapter 9).

Sample question

Could you answer this question? Below is a typical problem question that could arise on this topic. Guidelines on answering the question are included at the end of the chapter, whilst a sample essay question and guidance on tackling it can be found on the companion website.

Problem question

After an argument, Davy is burning his sister's collection of postcards in a small fire he started at the bottom of the garden. After he walks away from the smouldering embers, a spark from the fire sets light to the neighbour's wooden fence. Donald watches the fence burn but does nothing.

Discuss the criminal liability of Davy and Donald.

■ Criminal damage

KEY STATUTORY PROVISION

Criminal Damage Act 1971, s.1(1)

A person who without lawful excuse destroys or damages any property belonging to another intending to destroy or damage any such property or being reckless as to whether any such property would be destroyed or damaged shall be guilty of an offence.

Four *actus reus* elements	Two *alternative mens rea* elements
Destruction/damage	Intention to damage/destroy property belonging to another
Property	
Belonging to another	*or*
Without lawful excuse	Recklessness thereto

Actus reus elements

Damage or destruction

Section 1(1) covers two types of harm to property:

■ *Damage*: material change affecting the value and/or utility of the property, i.e. ripping pages from a book; and
■ *Destruction*: total elimination of value/utility that renders the property wholly useless, i.e. putting a book through a shredder.

REVISION NOTE

Although damage/destruction usually results from a postive act, i.e. setting fire to a house, it can arise from failure to act, i.e. dropping a cigarette and ignoring the resultant fire. Revisit Chapter 2 to refresh your memory on liability for omissions, particularly creation of dangerous situations.

Property

The definition of 'property' found in CDA, s.10 is similar to that used in theft (Chapter 13) with two exceptions in that the criminal damage definition:

1 excludes intangible property such as credit balances; and
2 includes real property such as land and buildings. These cannot be stolen but are frequently the target of criminal damage.

Belonging to another

Criminal damage requires that property 'belongs to another'; it is *not* an offence to damage/destroy one's own property.

The aggravated offence does cover damage/destruction of one's own property; this is a key distinction between the two offences.

Lawful excuse

There is disagreement as to whether 'lawful excuse' is part of the *actus reus* of criminal damage or whether it is a defence that only comes into operation after the *actus reus* and *mens rea* are established. This chapter is not the place to pursue this issue but, as different lecturers will have their own views, check your course materials to find which approach they advocate. The overall outcome will be the same irrespective of whether lawful excuse is treated as part of the offence or as a defence.

> **KEY STATUTORY PROVISION**
>
> **Criminal Damage Act 1971, s.5(2)**
>
> **(a)** If at the time of the act[s]... he believed that the person[s] whom he believed to be entitled to consent to the destruction of or damage to the property... had so consented, or would have consented to it if he or they had known of the destruction or damage and its circumstances; or
>
> **(b)** If he had destroyed or damaged... the property... in order to protect property belonging to himself or another or a right or interest in property... and at the time of the act or acts alleged to constitute the offence he believed –
>
> **(i)** that the property, right or interest was in immediate need of protection; and
>
> **(ii)** that the means of protection adopted... were... reasonable having regard to all the circumstances.

Section 5 is a detailed provision but its essence is that there are two situations in which the defendant will have a lawful excuse to damage or destroy property:

1. He believed the owner *consented* to the damage/destruction or would have done had they known of the circumstances.
2. He destroyed/damaged property believing this to be the most reasonable way to *protect property* from immediate threat.

Consent: The belief that the owner would consent to the damage/destruction of property must be honestly-held but need not be reasonable. This can lead to seemingly-anomalous conclusions.

This area causes problems for students who focus on the reasonableness of the defendant's behaviour, rather than on the defendant's belief in consent. Consider:

(a) Delores breaks a window to enter Victoria's house, because she thinks that her missing child may be inside. Delores is afraid that Victoria will be furious about the broken window, suggesting that she believes Victoria would not have consented to the damage. Delores is unlikely to be able to rely on lawful excuse.

(b) Victor agrees to lend his golf clubs to Dennis and to leave his house keys 'in the usual place' so Dennis can collect them while he is out. Dennis cannot find the key so he smashes a window and leaves a note saying 'fancy forgetting to leave me the key. I'll help you sweep the glass up later'. The jokey tone of the note suggests that Dennis believes Victor will consent to the damage, therefore he may be able to rely on lawful excuse.

Most people would consider that Delores behaved more reasonably than Dennis, but this is irrelevant to whether they honestly believed the owner would consent to the damage. Focus on what the defendant believes rather than what you think about his behaviour and remember to take into account the following:

∎ An honestly-held belief need not be reasonable;
∎ It does not matter if the belief is mistaken, *i.e.* Dennis would still be able to rely on lawful excuse even if Victor was furious about the damage.

Protection of property: This is more complicated than lawful excuse based on consent. There are three requirements that must be satisfied:

1 There must be an *immediate threat* to property;
2 The steps taken to protect the property must be *reasonable*; and
3 The property must be damaged or destroyed *in order to protect it*.

KEY CASE

R v. *Hunt* (1977) 66 Cr App R 105

Concerning: lawful excuse, protection of property

Facts

The defendant was worried about inadequate fire-safety precautions in sheltered accommodation but his concerns were dismissed by the management. He started a fire in order to draw attention to the inoperable fire alarms and inadequacy of the evacuation procedures.

Legal principle

Lawful excuse was not available as the defendant was motivated by a desire to draw attention to safety defects rather than to protect property. The issue of whether actions were undertaken 'in order to protect property' was an objective question to be determined by the court with no regard for the defendant's motive or intentions.

This was affirmed in *Hill and Hall* (1988) Cr App R 74 which gave rise to a two-stage test based upon the statutory requirements (see Figure 12.1).

Figure 12.1

STAGE 1 – SUBJECTIVE
Did the defendant believe that the property was in immediate need of protection and that the means used to protect the property were reasonable?

STAGE 2 – OBJECTIVE
Was the defendants act performed in order to protect property?

Mens rea elements

Intention

Intentional damage/destruction of property is usually straightforward as the defendant's aim will be evident.

There must be intention in relation to all aspects of the *actus reus* so the defendant must intend to damage/destroy property *belonging to another*: a person who intentionally damages property believing that it is his own is not liable.

Recklessness

For many years, criminal damage was based on objective recklessness but, since the House of Lords overruled *Caldwell* [1982] AC 341, the test has been subjective.

REVISION NOTE

R v. *G* is covered in Chapter 3. It has profound implications on criminal damage so make sure that you understand the new subjective *mens rea* test.

Remember, all cases decided using *Caldwell* recklessness were based on the now-obsolete objective test of recklessness.

KEY DEFINITION

Recklessness A person acts recklessly... with respect to –

(i) a circumstance when he is aware of a risk that it exists or will exist;
(ii) a result when he is aware of a risk that it will occur;

and it is, in the circumstances known to him, unreasonable to take the risk (*R* v. *G* [2004] 1 AC 1034).

There are three points to note:

1 This test of recklessness is based on volitional risk-taking therefore the defendant must be aware that there is a risk that property belonging to another will be damaged.
2 It is irrelevant that the defendant thinks that the risk of damage is very small; it is awareness of a risk that is the basis of recklessness, not awareness of the magnitude of the risk.
3 *R* v. *G* differs from other forms of subjective recklessness as it contains explicit references to 'reasonable' risk-taking.

Problem area: reasonable risk-taking

R v. *G* recklessness acknowledges that not all risk-taking is unreasonable and that liability only attaches to unreasonable risk-taking. This involves consideration of the:

▮ probability of the harm occurring; and
▮ social utility of the defendant's conduct.

For example, a person who swerves whilst driving and hits a wall will be viewed as reckless if he did so because his attention was distracted by his CD-player. This has no social utility and relatively high risk. However, if he swerved to avoid a child who had run into the road, the higher social utility is likely to render this a reasonable risk.

This illustrates that it is the circumstances surrounding the defendant's actions that are important when assessing the reasonableness of his risk-taking rather than the action itself. Look at the facts in a problem question for evidence of social utility and the level of probability of harm occuring in order to evaluate whether the defendant has taken an unreasonable risk, i.e. whether he has been reckless for the purposes of criminal damage. (*R* v. *G* only applies to criminal damage.)

▮ Aggravated criminal damage

KEY STATUTORY PROVISION

Criminal Damage Act 1971, s.1(2)

A person who without lawful excuse destroys or damages any property, whether belonging to himself or another –

(a) Intending to destroy or damage any property or being reckless as to whether any property would be destroyed or damaged; and
(b) Intending by the destruction or damage to endanger the life of another or being reckless as to whether the law of another would be thereby endangered

is guilty of an offence.

Aggravated criminal damage differs in two ways to the basic offence; one relating to the *mens rea* and the other to the *actus reus* of the offence (see Figure 12.2).

Figure 12.2

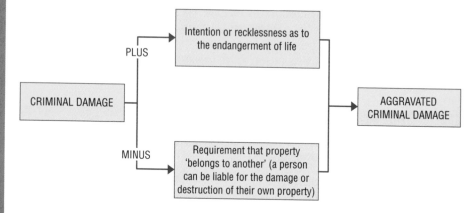

Actus reus elements

Belonging to another

In general, a person may do anything they wish with their own property, including destroying or damaging it; however, to do so in such a way that the lives of others are endangered attracts criminal liability.

Mens rea elements

Endangerment of life

The major distinction between the basic and aggravated offences lies with the requirement that the defendant *intends* or is *reckless* as to the *endangerment of life*:

■ There is no need for life to be endangered. This is a *mens rea* element so concerns the defendant's state of mind not his actions.
■ The defendant must intend that life is endangered by the damage/destruction of property (or be reckless thereto).

KEY CASE

R v. *Steer* [1987] 2 All ER 833

Concerning: endangerment of life

Facts
As a result of a grudge against his former business partner, the defendant fired a rifle at the windows of his house, causing damage. Nobody inside the house was injured. The defendant's conviction for criminal damage with intent to endanger life was quashed by the House of Lords.

Legal principle
It must be the damage to property that endangers life not the means by which the property is damaged. Therefore, the defendant must have intended to endanger life by smashing windows or foreseen a risk that life would be endangered by smashing windows. The means by which the windows were smashed – firing a rifle – and the life-endangering potential of this method of damaging property were irrelevant and could not be used as a basis for liability.

It is not enough that the defendant's act causes criminal damage and endangers life; the defendant must intend or foresee that the criminal damage caused by his act will endanger life.

FURTHER THINKING

The distinction that the courts have made between 'endangerment by criminal damage' and 'endangerment by the means used to cause criminal damage' has been criticised as a 'dismal distinction'. If you want to explore this further, as preparation for an essay, there is an excellent critical evaluation of the distinction and its implications: Elliot, D.W. 'Endangering Life by Destroying or Damaging Property' [1997] *Criminal Law Review* 382.

Arson

KEY STATUTORY PROVISION

Criminal Damage Act 1971, s.1(3)

An offence committed under this section by destroying or damaging property by fire shall be charged as arson.

This offence replicates criminal damage when the means used to damage/destroy property is fire.

Chapter summary:
Putting it all together

☐ Can you tick all the points from the revision checklist at the beginning of this chapter?

☐ Take the **end-of-chapter quiz** on the companion website.

☐ Test your knowledge of the cases with the **revision flashcards** on the website.

☐ Attempt the problem question from the beginning of the chapter using the guidelines below.

☐ Go to the companion website to try out other questions.

Answer guidelines

See the problem question at the start of the chapter. A diagram illustrating how to structure your answer is available on the website.

Points to remember when answering this question

■ As the property is destroyed by fire, the charge is arson (CDA, s.1(3)).

■ Davy has destroyed (a) his sister's postcards and (b) his neighbour's fence. These should be dealt with separately as his *mens rea* will differ, i.e. he burned the postcards deliberately (intention) but the fence accidentally (recklessness).

■ Donald has not done anything but you are asked to consider his liability so consider whether he has a duty to act giving rise to liability by omission. Even if your conclusion is that he has no duty and no liability, there are still marks to be gained in reaching this conclusion.

Make your answer really stand out

■ Make effective use of the facts. For example, as Davy has argued with his sister, it is likely that he is burning her postcards to upset her so there is no basis for arguments of lawful excuse based on consent. If the question did not specify that there was an argument, it would be reasonable to consider whether he might have permission to burn the postcards.

■ The omissions argument provides greatest scope to impress the examiner. A weak answer would state that Donald has no liability as he has not done anything. A better answer would outline the categories of duty to act but conclude that Donald does not fall within them. An excellent answer would probe deeper and consider whether Donald could fall within one of the categories of duty. Ask the question, *who is Donald?* Is he Davy's friend who helped him start the fire (creating a dangerous situation) or is he the neighbour's gardener (potential duty to act based on contract).

13
Theft

THEFT	
Section 1(1) Theft Act 1968	

Actus reus	Mens rea
Appropriation (s.3) Property (s.4) Belonging to another (s.5)	Dishonesty (s.2 and *Ghosh* test) Intention permanently to deprive (s.6)

Revision checklist

What you need to know:

☐ *Actus reus* and *mens rea* of theft

☐ Difficulties associated with the ownership, possession and transfer of property

☐ Implications for theft of judicial interpretation of 'appropriation'

☐ The *Ghosh* test of dishonesty

☐ The 'thought rather than action' nature of intention permanently to deprive

Introduction:
Understanding theft

There is a surprising gap between the legal meaning of theft and the everyday understanding of the word.

This always causes problems for students who struggle to understand why situations that 'feel' like theft attract no liability under the Theft Act 1968 whilst other situations that they do not think of as theft, such as reclaiming one's own property, fall foul of the law. This mismatch leads many students astray as they apply their instinctive evaluation of theft and reach erroneous conclusions. The advice 'follow the legal rules and accept the conclusion they produce' is frequently ignored but is really the key to success in this area of law.

Essay question advice

Essays on theft can take a variety of forms. They could require a consideration of the offence as a whole, examine the overlap between theft and other offences, particularly obtaining property by deception (Chapter 15) or focus on a narrow issue, such as appropriation. Make sure that you only tackle a narrowly-drawn essay if you have sufficient depth of knowledge: there is no point in answering a question on dishonesty if all you can do is state the *Ghosh* test.

Sample question

Could you answer this question? Below is a typical problem question that could arise on this topic. Guidelines on answering the question are included at the end of the chapter, whilst a sample essay question and guidance on tackling it can be found on the companion website.

Problem question

Dan goes to his tutor's office to return a book he borrowed. The room is empty but the door is open so Dan goes inside. He sees another copy of the same book and thinks that the tutor probably has several so decides not to return the copy he has been using. He also spots an exam paper on the desk and leans across to read the questions. Later, confident about his success in the coming exam, he tells his grandmother, who is easily confused, that he has already taken it and gained top marks, hoping that she will reward him with a laptop as she has promised. She gives him £500.

Discuss Dan's liability for theft.

■ Theft

KEY STATUTORY PROVISION

Theft Act 1968, s.1(1)

A person is guilty of theft if he dishonestly appropriates property belonging to another with the intention of permanently depriving the other of it.

Three *actus reus* elements	Two *mens rea* elements
Appropriation	Dishonesty
Property	Intention permanently to deprive
Belonging to another	

Actus reus elements

Property

KEY STATUTORY PROVISION

Theft Act 1968, s.4(1)

Property includes money and all other property, real or personal, including things in action and other intangible property.

Figure 13.1

Things which amount to property	Things which do not amount to property
• Money (coins, notes, currency) • Real property • Personal property (any tangible object that is not real property) • Things in action (something that cannot be seen but which can be enforced by legal action: see Chapter 15)	• Land: s.4(2) • Mushrooms, flowers, fruit and foliage growing wild: s.4(3) • Wild creatures, tamed or untamed: s.4(4) • Confidential information: *Oxford* v. *Moss* (1979) 68 Crim App R 183 • Corpses: *Kelly* [1999] QB 621

Problems rarely arise with tangible property, i.e. things with physical presence that can be touched, although money always causes confusion. Intangible property such as things in action can also be troublesome (see Figure 13.1).

EXAM TIP

If the property element of theft is straightforward in a problem question, do not complicate it for the sake of demonstrating what you know. Discussion of issues not raised by the question attract no credit. For example, if the question involves the defendant taking the victim's credit card, it would suffice to state 'the card is personal property within the meaning of s.4': there is no need to mention a thing in action unless the card is used.

Belonging to another

> **Theft Act, 1968, s.5(1)**
>
> Property shall be regarded as belonging to any person having possession or control of it, or having in it any proprietary right or interest.
>
> *KEY STATUTORY PROVISION*

This definition indicates that 'belonging to another' includes situations short of outright ownership, such as possession of property. This is usually straightforward although it can lead to the conclusion that the defendant is liable for theft of his own property if he removes it from someone who is in lawful possession of it: *Turner* [1971] WLR 901.

Statute also provides two further situations that can be complicated:

1 property given for a particular purpose
2 property passed by mistake.

First consider particular purpose.

> **Theft Act 1968, s.5(3)**
>
> Where a person has received property from or on account of another and is under an obligation to the other to retain and deal with that property or its proceeds in a particular way, the property or proceeds shall be regarded... as belonging to another.
>
> *KEY STATUTORY PROVISION*

Section 5(3) deals with situations whereby the defendant has been given property, frequently money, for a particular purpose but has used it in a different way. In such circumstances, the property is regarded as belonging to the original owner.

Problem area: segregation of funds

In *Hall* [1973] QB 126, it was held that a travel agent who received payments from customers but did not use this to purchase holidays on their behalf could not be liable for theft because he had paid the money into his general trading account. This mingling of property meant that there was no ascertainable property that had remained in the ownership of the customer. Money could only fall within s.5(3) if it was kept separately as this denoted that it was received for a particular purpose.

This requirement was doubted in *Wain* [1995] 2 Cr App R 660 in which the defendant kept money donated to charity for himself and claimed he was not liable for theft as the donations had been mingled with his own money. The court held that the requirement for segregation of funds created a false distinction between a collector who received money in a collection box (who would be liable if he kept the money) and one who mingled it with his own money (who would not be liable). It was held that anyone who collects money for charity should be liable if he keeps it for his own use.

Wain could be seen as rejecting the need for segregation of funds entirely, in which case *Hall* would now be decided differently, or it could be limited in application to situations involving money collected for charity.

If a problem question raises s.5(3) in the context of charitable donations, *Wain* should be followed. In any other circumstances, both *Hall* and *Wain* should be applied with an explanation that the case law is unclear on this point and the result would depend on which line of authority was preferred by the courts in subsequent cases.

Next consider property received by mistake.

KEY STATUTORY PROVISION

Theft Act 1968, s.5(4)

Where a person gets property by another's mistake and is under an obligation to make restoration. . . of the property or its proceeds. . . then [this] shall be regarded. . . as belonging to the person entitled to restoration and an intention not to make restoration shall be regarded accordingly as an intention to deprive that person of the property or proceeds.

Section 5(4) provides that property (again, usually money) which is passed to the defendant by mistake is regarded as 'belonging to' the original owner. This means that failure to return the property once the mistake has been realised amounts to theft.

The failure must be deliberate so the defendant must be aware that he has received property by mistake. For example, in *Attorney-General's Reference (No 1 of 1983)* [1985] QB 182, a computer error led to an overpayment of wages into the defendant's account which she noticed but failed to return, giving rise to liability for theft. Had she failed to notice the overpayment, she would not have been liable.

Appropriation

KEY STATUTORY PROVISION

Theft Act 1968, s.3(1)

Any assumption by a person of the rights of the owner amounts to an appropriation and this includes, where he has come by the property (innocently or not) without stealing it, any later assumption of a right to it by keeping it or dealing with it as owner.

This definition raises three questions:

- What are the rights of the owner?
- Do all of them have to be assumed for appropriation to take place?
- Is there still an appropriation if the owner consents to the appropriation of his rights?

Bundles of rights

The owner of property has the right to do anything with it. The owner of a book can read it, throw it away, write in it or destroy it. It is because property can be used in a whole range of ways that ownership carries a bundle of different rights over property (which includes unusual uses, i.e. the owner of a book could bury it in the garden).

Assumption of rights

It is because ownership conveys a bundle of rights that appropriation is satisfied by the assumption of *any* of the rights rather than *all* of the rights of ownership: *Morris* [1984] AC 320. A defendant who reads a book belonging to another, writes in it or destroys is has committed the *actus reus* of theft just as much as a defendant who has treated it in a way that is more consistent with everyday notions of theft, i.e. taken it out of the owner's possession.

Consent

There was conflict in case law as to whether the owner's consent to the property being taken negates appropriation which was settled in *Gomez* (see Figure 13.2).

Figure 13.2

Lawrence v. *MPC* [1972] AC 626

A foreign passenger who was unfamiliar with the currency handed his wallet to a taxi driver to enable him to take the fare. The driver removed money greatly in excess of the correct fare. He argued that this could not amount to an appropriation because the owner consented to the removal of his property.

The House of Lords rejected this argument and held that the question was whether the rights of the owner had been assumed and the issue of consent was irrelevant.

CONFLICT

Morris [1984] AC 320

The defendant switched the labels on goods in a supermarket in order to pay a lower price for the goods. He was apprehended prior to making payment and leaving the shop. It was argued that there was no appropriation because the goods had been picked up and handled with the implied consent of the owner.

The House of Lords held that appropriation implied that there was an adverse usurpation of the owners rights therefore it was something that only happened if the owner did not consent to that assumption of his rights.

DPP v. *Gomez* [1993] 1 All ER 1

The defendant was the assistant manager of an electrical goods shop who accepted worthless cheques. He told the manager that the cheques were valid so the manager authorised the release of property valued at £16,000. The defendant argued that he could not be liable for theft because the manager consented to the removal of the property.

The House of Lords addressed the conflict between the previous cases and chose to follow *Lawrence*, holding that consent is not relevant to the question of appropriation.

Note: *Morris* was overruled on this point but is still good law for the proposition that assumption of any one of the rights of the owner amounts to appropriation.

FURTHER THINKING

Here we start to see how the legal definition differs from everyday understanding of theft. As appropriation is the assumption of any of the rights of the owner, even if the owner consents to this assumption, the *actus reus* of theft is satisfied every time we do something with someone else's property. In other words, we all commit the *actus reus* of theft all the time!

The only difference between lawful behaviour and theft rests in the *mens rea*. This is a particular problem in relation to gifts as part of the *mens rea* is also satisfied: the intention permanently to deprive. If the only remaining element of theft – dishonesty – is satisfied then the recipient of the gift will be liable for theft.

The following article provides a clear overview of the consequences of the wide interpretation of appropriation adopted in *Gomez* and its consequences in cases involving gifts so would be useful reading in preparation for an essay on this topic: Shute, S., 'Appropriation and the Law of Theft' [2002] *Criminal Law Review* 445.

R v. *Hinks* [2000] 3 WLR 1590

Concerning: appropriation, gifts

Facts

The defendant encouraged the victim, a man of limited intelligence, to withdraw money from the building society and deposit it in her account. She contended that these were valid gifts but was nonetheless convicted of theft.

Legal principle

The House of Lords held that, following *Gomez*, receipt of a gift that amounted to a valid transfer of ownership at civil law could still amount to theft if it was dishonestly induced by the defendant.

Mens rea elements

Dishonesty

Theft Act 1968, s.2(1)

A person's appropriation of property is not to be regarded as dishonesty:

(a) if he appropriates property in the belief that he has in law the right to deprive the other of it, on behalf of himself or of a third party;

(b) if he appropriates property in the belief that he would have had the other's consent if the other knew of the appropriation and the circumstances of it; or

(c) if he appropriates property in the belief that the person to whom the property belongs cannot be discovered by taking reasonable steps.

This is not a definition of dishonesty but a statement of situations that are *not* dishonest. They are all subjective tests so are determined on the basis of what the defendant believed irrespective of how others would interpret the situation. If none of these situations apply, the general test of dishonesty outlined in *Ghosh* should be applied.

KEY CASE

R v. *Ghosh* [1982] QB 1053

Concerning: dishonesty

Facts

The defendant was a surgeon who claimed fees for operations that were carried out by other surgeons which should have attracted no fee (because they were on NHS patients). He asserted that he believed he was entitled to the fees so was not dishonest.

Legal principle

The Court of Appeal held that, outside of s.2, dishonesty could not be assessed on a purely subjective standard and formulated a two-stage test:

1 Was what was done dishonest according to the ordinary standards of reasonable and honest people?
2 Did the defendant realise that reasonable and honest people regard what he did as dishonest?

If the answer to both questions is 'yes', the defendant is dishonest. If the answer to either question is 'no', the defendant is not dishonest.

EXAM TIP

It is common for students to misstate the *Ghosh* test. As dishonesty is part of every theft problem as well as questions on other property offences (Chapters 14 and 15), it is essential to be able to state the test correctly and apply it to the facts. Remember, though, to apply the negative definition from s.2 *before* the *Ghosh* test (see Figure 13.3).

Intention permanently to deprive

KEY STATUTORY PROVISION

Theft Act 1968, s.6(1)

A person. . . is regarded as having the intention of permanently depriving. . . if his intention is to treat the thing as his own to dispose of regardless of the other's rights. . . [B]orrowing or lending. . . may amount to so treating it if, but only if, the borrowing or lending is for a period and in circumstances making it equivalent to an outright taking or disposal.

Figure 13.3

STAGE 1 – NEGATIVE DEFINITION
Consider whether the defendant falls within any of the three situations contained in s.2. Look for evidence that he believed:
(a) he was legally (rather than morally) entitled to take the property
(b) that the owner would agree to him taking the property if they knew
(c) that the owner could not be found by taking reasonable steps.
Remember that these must be honestly-held beliefs but they do not have to be accurate.

If any of the negative definitions are satisfied, the defendant is not dishonest and cannot be liable for theft. If none of the s.2 situations apply, go on to apply the *Ghosh* test.

STAGE 2 – *GHOSH* TEST
Provide an accurate statement of the *Ghosh* test and apply it to the facts to establish dishonesty.
(1) The first stage is objective so consider what 'reasonable and honest' people would think about the defendant's conduct. This is often a matter of making generalisations about social standards of honesty: most people view taking property from shops without paying is dishonest.
(2) The second stage is based upon what the defendant thinks about ordinary standards of honesty. Is he aware that 'reasonable and honest' people would consider his conduct to be dishonest even though he thinks that it is acceptable? Look for evidence of surreptitious behaviour in the facts: a defendant who sneaks out or hides goods cannot believe that ordinary people would believe that he was being honest.

Section 6(1) includes situations where the property is taken on a temporary basis (borrowing) so goes beyond what might ordinarily be thought of as permanent deprivation.

KEY CASE

R v. *Lloyd* [1985] QB 829

Concerning: borrowing, intention permanently to deprive

Facts

The defendant worked at a cinema and removed films so that pirate copies could be made. The copying process took a few hours, after which the films were returned. He appealed against his conviction for theft on the basis that he intended only temporary deprivation.

Legal principle

The Court of Appeal held that borrowing would amount to outright taking only where the property was returned in such a changed state that all its goodness and virtue were gone. The partial diminution of value represented by the copying of the films would not suffice despite the reduction in revenue caused by the availability of pirate films.

EXAM TIP

One of the commonest mistakes is to focus on whether the property was actually taken on a permanent basis. This leads to inaccurate conclusions. Not only can borrowing satisfy the intention permanently to deprive but situations that involve only a transient interference with another's property can give rise to liability, i.e. picking up goods in a shop intending to steal them but having a change of heart and leaving without them. This is because intention permanently to deprive is concerned with the defendant's state of mind, not his actions. Consider what the defendant's intentions were at the time he appropriated the property: if it was to remove it permanently then his liability is established irrespective of what he actually went on to do.

Chapter summary:
Putting it all together

☐ Can you tick all the points from the revision checklist at the beginning of this chapter?

☐ Take the **end-of-chapter quiz** on the companion website.

☐ Test your knowledge of the cases with the **revision flashcards** on the website.

☐ Attempt the problem question from the beginning of the chapter using the guidelines below.

☐ Go to the companion website to try out other questions

Answer guidelines

See the problem question at the start of the chapter. A diagram illustrating how to structure your answer is available on the website.

Points to remember when answering this question

▮ Discuss each of the three incidents separately. Never be tempted to merge events even if it conserves words or time. Your answer will be really confused if you start with property and apply it to all three events.

▮ Remember to argue both ways wherever possible and make reference to the facts. This is particularly important in relation to dishonesty with regard to the book and the £500.

Make your answer really stand out

▮ Remember the key cases and make sure that these are included to support your answer whenever appropriate.

▮ Provide an accurate statement of the *Ghosh* test: it is done inaccurately so often that precision here will really impress your examiner.

14
Theft-related offences

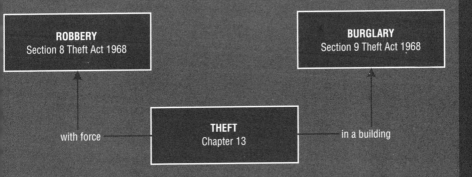

Revision checklist

What you need to know:

☐ *Actus reus* and *mens rea* of the offences
☐ The relationship between theft and burglary/robbery
☐ The 'continuing act' approach to appropriation in robbery
☐ Distinction between the two forms of burglary

Introduction:
Understanding theft-related offences

Certain situations in which theft occurs are regarded as more serious so form the subject-matter of separate offences.

Robbery involves the use of force to facilitate the theft whereas burglary involves the intrusion into property, domestic or residential, in order to steal. Burglary also has manifestations involving criminal damage and GBH which are often overlooked.

The problems arising from these offences are similar to the problems associated with theft: robbery and burglary are terms used in everyday life which bear only a passing resemblance to their legal meaning. It is essential that you disregard your preconceived understandings of these offences and focus instead on the legal definition of the elements of the robbery and burglary.

Essay question advice

Essays on theft-related offences are uncommon but may arise either separately or in combination with theft. The important thing to remember is to focus on addressing the issue raised in the question rather than merely describing the elements of the offences.

Theft-related problems often combine theft with deception but can arise with any other offences and defences. Look for 'clues' in the answer that trigger these offences: 'theft with force' (robbery) and 'theft in a building' (burglary) but also remember that burglary is not limited to theft but includes criminal damage and GBH.

Sample question

Could you answer this question? Below is a typical problem question that could arise on this topic. Guidelines on answering the question are included at the end of the chapter, whilst a sample essay question and guidance on tackling it can be found on the companion website.

Problem question

Dan taps an elderly lady on the arm to attract her attention and asks directions to the town centre. Whilst she is pointing and her attention is distracted, he removes her purse from her bag without her noticing. Dan decides to steal a bottle of wine from the off-licence. He hides the wine under his coat but is spotted by the shopkeeper who tries to stop him leaving so Dan trips him over breaking his leg.

Discuss Dan's liability.

◼ Robbery

KEY STATUTORY PROVISION

Theft Act 1968, s.8(1)

A person is guilty of robbery if he steals, and immediately before or at the time of doing so, and in order to do so, he uses force on any person or puts or seeks to put any person in fear of being then and there subjected to force.

Actus reus elements	*Mens rea* elements
Actus reus of theft	*Mens rea* of theft
Force (or fear of force)	Intentional use of force
To any person	
At the time or immediately before the theft	

Actus reus elements

The *actus reus* elements can be encapsulated by answering four questions about robbery (see Figure 14.1).

Figure 14.1

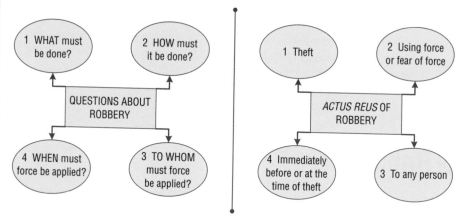

Theft

As robbery is an aggravated form of theft, all the elements of theft must be present in order for robbery to be established.

Force/fear of force

There are four points to remember:

1 The level of force may be minimal, e.g. pushing/jostling (*Dawson* (1976) 64 Cr App R 170) as well as more serious violence.
2 Force may be applied to the person or their property, e.g. grabbing a handbag without touching the owner (*Clouden* [1987] Crim LR 56).

3 Fear of force will suffice. Look out for express ('give me that or else') or implied threats (menacing behaviour) that have induced fear in the victim.
4 Force must be used to facilitate theft. The essence of robbery is that force is used to commit theft so there must be a causal link between the theft and the force used.

EXAM TIP

The fourth point can cause confusion as students tend to take a mathematical approach:

$$FORCE + THEFT = ROBBERY$$

This can be a useful way to remember the requirements of robbery but it is not always strictly accurate. Imagine the defendant knocks the victim to the ground intending to rape her. She offers him money to leave her alone and he takes it. This would amount to theft and he has subjected her to force but it would not amount to robbery. This is because he used force in order to rape *not* in order to steal.

As such, it is more useful to remember the offence as:

$$FORCE \text{ (used to commit) } THEFT = ROBBERY$$

Any person

Force is often used on the owner of the property but the reference to 'any person' in s.8 means that this need not be the case. Robbery would be too narrow if it was restricted to force used against the owner of property as this would exclude, for example, bank robbery whereby the employees are threatened but clearly are not the owners of the money.

Immediately before or at the time

As robbery requires that force is used in order to steal, the use of force must precede or coincide with the theft. Force used after the theft is complete cannot have been instrumental in committing theft.

Despite the logic of this position, it limited the scope of robbery by placing situations in which the defendant used violence to get away after theft outside the offence.

R v. *Hale* (1978) 68 Cr App R 415

Concerning: timing of force

Facts

The defendant's accomplice stole jewellery whilst the defendant remained downstairs with the owner of the house. He tied her to a chair and threatened to harm her child if she called the police after they left. He argued that the force occurred after the theft so he could not be liable for robbery.

Legal principle

Appropriation is a continuing act that commences with the first assumption of the owner's rights but which does not cease immediately (the duration of appropriation is a question of fact for the jury).

EXAM TIP

Do not dismiss situations in which force is used *after* theft is complete without considering whether there is a continuing appropriation. If after applying *Hale* you conclude there is no robbery, the defendant may still be liable for theft and a non-fatal offence (Chapters 9 and 10).

Mens rea elements

This combines the *mens rea* of theft with an intention to use force in order to steal.

Burglary

Theft Act 1968, s.9(1)

A person is guilty of burglary if –

(a) He enters any building or part of a building as a trespasser and with intent to commit any such offence as mentioned in subsection (2) below; or

(b) Having entered any building or part of a building as a trespasser he steals or attempts to steal... inflicts or attempts to inflict on any person therein grievous bodily harm.

Actus reus elements	*Mens rea* elements
Entry	Intention/recklessness as to trespass
Building (or part of)	Ulterior intent (s.9(1)(a) only)
As a trespasser	
Actual offence (s.9(1)(b) only)	

This creates two separate offences with some common elements (see Figure 14.2).

Figure 14.2

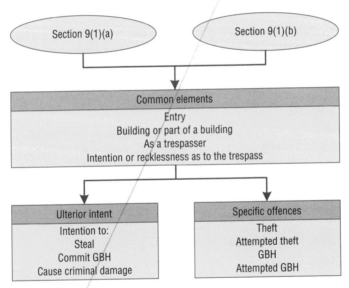

Common elements

Entry

▌ Straightforward if the defendant's whole body is in the building.
▌ Partial entry will suffice, e.g. the defendant's arm is through a window: *Brown* [1985] Crim LR 212.
▌ Entry is deemed if the defendant remains outside but uses an instrument to remove property or sends an innocent agent to commit an offence: *Wellhouse* [1994] Crim LR 756.

Building or part of a building

Buildings are usually straightforward but there are two tricky areas:

1 Non-typical structures. Section 9(4) specifies that inhabited vehicles and vessels are within the meaning of 'building'. Other structures are judged according to whether they are of sufficient size and permanence: *Stevens* v. *Gurley* (1859) 7 CB 99.
2 Separate areas within a building such as individual rooms in a multiple-occupancy house and 'staff only' areas in shops.

KEY CASE

R v. *Walkington* [1979] 2 All ER 716

Concerning: part of a building

Facts

The defendant went behind a shop counter and interfered with the till. He argued that he was not liable for burglary as he had not formed the intention to steal before entering the shop and that the till area was not a separate 'part of a building'.

Legal principle

It was held that a part of a building was determined by the presence of a physical demarcation such as separate rooms, notices restricting entry or some form of barrier such as a counter.

As a trespasser

KEY CASE

R v. *Collins* [1973] QB 100

Concerning: trespass

Facts

The defendant, naked apart from his socks, climbed a ladder and looked through the victim's bedroom window. She assumed it was her boyfriend and beckoned him into the room. She realised her mistake during intercourse. He was charged with s.9(1)(a) burglary which, at the time, included intention to rape within the ulterior intent.

Legal principle

Trespass requires entry without permission so if the defendant believed he had permission to enter prior to any part of his body crossing the threshold then he would not be a trespasser and cannot be liable for burglary.

This highlights the dual aspects of trespass in burglary:

- entry into a building (or part of) without permission: *actus reus*
- knowledge that there is no permission or awareness that there is a risk that there is no permission to enter: *mens rea*.

Permission to enter may be express or implied and may be limited to particular parts of the building or to entry for a specific purpose. For example, permission to enter a hotel may include the lounge but will exclude the kitchens. A person who exceeds the extent of his permission may still be a trespasser.

KEY CASE

R v. *Jones and Smith* [1976] 63 Cr App R 47

Concerning: exceeding permission to enter

Facts

The defendant entered his father's house with a friend to steal two televisions. He had general permission to enter the house and argued that this meant that he was not a trespasser for the purposes of burglary.

Legal principle

It was held that a person who enters a building for an unlawful purpose will be a trespasser in that building irrespective of any express or implied permission to entry that has been extended to him.

EXAM TIP

Trespass is a tort (civil wrong). It is *not* a criminal offence yet students frequently comment on the defendant's liability for trespass (possibly because of the misleading signs which state 'trespassers will be prosecuted'). As the following case demonstrates, trespass cannot give rise to criminal liability unless the other elements of burglary are present:

Laing [1995] Crim LR 395, the defendant was found in the stockroom of a shop after closing time. He had not stolen anything or attempted to do so and there was no evidence that he had ulterior intent when entering either the shop or the stockroom. He was undoubtedly a trespasser but without the other elements of burglary there was no basis upon which he could be criminally liable.

Remember this and avoid making a common fundamental error that would really damage your answer.

Ulterior intent

In addition to these common elements, s.9(1)(a) requires an ulterior intent to commit theft, GBH or criminal damage *at the time that the defendant entered the building.* If the intent is not present upon entry, subsequent formation of ulterior intent will not amount to burglary.

EXAM TIP

Focus on what was in the defendant's mind at his point of entry into the building. Conditional intent will suffice: if the defendant intended to steal only if he could find something of value this will satisfy the ulterior intent requirement: *Attorney-General's Reference (Nos 1 and 2 of 1979)* [1980] QB 180.

This can be applied to the other offences:

■ Does the defendant intend to cause harm if a particular person is in the building?
■ Does the defendant intend to smash particular property if he can find it?

Remember that there is no need for the defendant to *do* anything; it is his intention that is crucial to liability, not his actions.

Specific offences

Section 9(1)(b) requires actual or attempted offending once the defendant is within the building so he must either satisfy:

■ all five elements of theft (Chapter 13), or
■ the elements of OAPA, s.20 (Chapter 10);

or

■ the requirements for liability for attempting either offence (Chapter 4).

EXAM TIP

Problem questions may give rise to liability for more than one offence of burglary in order to test your ability to distinguish between s.9(1)(a) and (b) offences. Spend some time untangling the facts and working through the elements of the offences to ensure you select the appropriate offences as the basis for liability.

Chapter summary:
Putting it all together

☐ Can you tick all the points from the revision checklist at the beginning of this chapter?

☐ Take the **end-of-chapter quiz** on the companion website.

☐ Test your knowledge of the cases with the **revision flashcards** on the website.

☐ Attempt the problem question from the beginning of the chapter using the guidelines below.

☐ Go to the companion website to try out other questions.

Answer guidelines

See the problem question at the start of the chapter. A diagram illustrating how to structure your answer is available on the website.

Points to remember when answering this question

■ The question appears to focus on robbery but careful analysis reveals that it raises two issues of burglary too. Remember that 'theft-in-a-building' should trigger a discussion of burglary and you can gain credit for spotting this easily-overlooked issue.

■ Using force 'in order to steal' is important to both robberies here: question why Dan tapped the old lady's arm and remember the issue of continuing appropriation in relation to the wine.

■ Incorporate key cases into your answer and use these to support your conclusions.

■ An answer plan may help you work in a methodical way. An example which deals with one robbery and one burglary element of the question is provided on the companion website.

Make your answer really stand out

■ The broken leg is GBH so triggers a discussion of s.9(1)(b) burglary. Impress your examiner by noting all manifestations of burglary not just those relating to theft.

■ Do not neglect the elements of the specified offences when establishing liability for s.9(1)(b): you should establish the liability for (a) theft and (b) GBH as part of establishing liability for burglary.

15
Deception offences

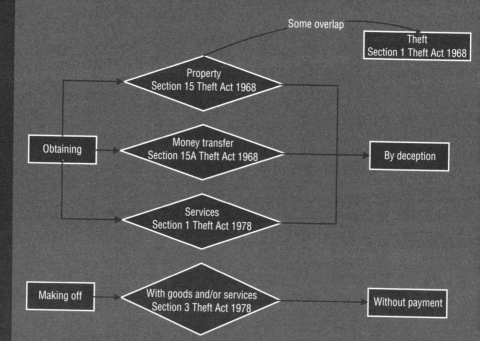

Some overlap

Theft
Section 1 Theft Act 1968

Property
Section 15 Theft Act 1968

Obtaining

Money transfer
Section 15A Theft Act 1968

By deception

Services
Section 1 Theft Act 1978

Making off

With goods and/or services
Section 3 Theft Act 1978

Without payment

Revision checklist

What you need to know:

- [ ] *Actus reus* and *mens rea* of the offences
- [ ] The relationships between the offences (including theft) and any overlap
- [ ] Manifestations of deceptive behaviour
- [ ] Relevance of timing regarding transfer of ownership
- [ ] Operation of financial transactions

Introduction:
Understanding deception offences

Deception offences differ from theft as they involve trickery to persuade others to part with their property.

These offences focus on the use of deception by the defendant to obtain a range of things (property, services, money transfers) to which he is not entitled. However, there is still a strong relationship with theft (Chapter 13) that you will need to bear in mind.

The offences are not particularly difficult in themselves but students can become puzzled over which offence to use in any particular situation. One way to resolve this is by focusing on the nature of the 'thing' that has been obtained (as demonstrated in the topic map above) although this will not always solve the problem. It is crucial to bear in mind the timing of the deception in relation to the transfer of property and this can also cause problems.

Essay question advice

Essays on deception are not common but can arise particularly if there have been recent developments in the law. Remember that deception may overlap with theft so look out for questions involving both offences.

Problem question advice

Deception offences, with or without theft, arise frequently in problems. They tend not to raise complicated legal issues but usually involve tangled facts which need to be unravelled to ascertain what the defendant did and when he did it in order to identify the relevant offence.

Sample question

Could you answer this question? Below is a typical problem question that could arise on this topic. Guidelines on answering the question are included at the end of the chapter, whilst a sample essay question and guidance on tackling it can be found on the companion website.

Problem question

David uses his brother's credit card to buy new trainers. He goes to the gym and uses his brother's membership card to gain entry. David had promised to buy Delilah lunch in an expensive restaurant but now has no means to pay. He orders a meal anyway. When the bill arrives, David shouts 'run' and races out of the restaurant followed by Delilah.

Discuss any criminal liability incurred by David and Delilah.

■ Obtaining property by deception

KEY STATUTORY PROVISION

Theft Act 1968, s.15

A person who by any deception dishonestly obtains property belonging to another, with the intention of permanently depriving the other of it, shall [be guilty of an offence].

Three *actus reus* elements	Three *mens rea* elements
Obtaining by deception	Dishonesty
Property	Intention permanently to deprive
Belonging to another	Intention/reckless as to deception

REVISION TIP

There is significant overlap between s.15 and theft so revisit Chapter 13 to remind yourself of the common elements. Note:

■ the negative definition of dishonesty (s.2) applies to theft, but not s.15
■ there is one additional *mens rea* requirement – intention/reckless as to deception.

If you have established liability for s.15, adding a sentence explaining the wide definition of appropriation in *Gomez* also gives rise to liability for theft is a simple way to demonstrate understanding and impress the examiner.

Actus reus elements

Given the overlap with theft, only 'obtaining by deception' remains to be discussed.

Obtaining by deception

This is an element of the first three offences discussed. It has two essential elements:

1 a false representation (deception)
2 that leads to the obtaining of property (causal link).

False representation is discussed first.

KEY STATUTORY PROVISION

Theft Act 1968, s.15(4)

'Deception' means any deception (whether deliberate or reckless) by words or conduct as to fact or as to law, including a deception as to the present intentions of the person using the deception or any other person.

This explains the scope of deception, i.e. that it includes words or conduct, but definition of deception was left to case law.

KEY DEFINITION

Deception To deceive is 'to induce a man to believe that a thing is true which is false and which the person practising the deceit knows or believes to be false' (*Re London and Globe Finance Ltd* [1903] 1 Ch 728).

Therefore, **deception** is an express or implied lie/falsehood which is presented as the truth by someone who knows it is (or may be) false.

EXAM TIP

In problems, examine the defendant's behaviour. Have they behaved as someone in their circumstances is expected to behave? For example, shoppers are expected to have appropriate means of payment whilst professionals are expected to follow the rules and practices of their profession. If a defendant's behaviour creates an impression that certain behaviour will follow but his actual behaviour is different, it is likely to amount to a false representation. Also, failure to correct an erroneous impression or to alert others to a relevant change in circumstances will amount to a false representation.

A false representation is not enough; it must cause the defendant to obtain property. To establish this causal link, the **deception** *must*:

■ occur *before* the property is obtained
■ be effective (it must deceive someone)
■ be operative (it must lead to the property being obtained).

KEY CASE

R v. *Doukas* [1978] 1 All ER 1061

Concerning: operative nature of deception

Facts

The defendant was a waiter who served his own wine to customers. This was an implied representation that the wine belonged to the hotel even though customers would not actually consider the ownership of the wine.

Legal principle

The question was not whether anyone had actively considered the question of ownership but whether they would have acted differently if they had known the true facts.

This four-question process is a good model to follow in **deception** problem questions (see Figure 15.1).

OBTAINING SERVICES BY DECEPTION

Figure 15.1

STAGE 1
Is there an express or implied false representation?

STAGE 2
Did this precede the obtaining of property?

STAGE 3
Has someone been deceived?

STAGE 4
Would they have behaved differently if they had known the truth?

EXAM TIP

Students generally cover false representation but often fail to go on to cover the need for a causal link. Strengthen your answer by addressing both points.

Emphasise this by using 'signposting' sentences. For example, 'in addition to establishing a false representation by the defendant, a link between this deception and obtaining of the property must be established'.

This will be even more successful if you replace 'the defendant' with the actual name used in the problem and 'the property' with that identified in the question.

Remember the importance of application of the law to the facts and strive to make your answers as specific in their use of the facts as possible.

■ Obtaining services by deception

KEY STATUTORY PROVISION

Theft Act 1978, s.1(1)

A person who by any deception dishonestly obtains services from another shall be guilty of an offence.

Two *actus reus* elements	Two *mens rea* elements
obtaining by deception	dishonesty
services	intention/recklessness as to deception

Compare the elements of this offence with obtaining property by deception. There are two missing elements:

1 belonging to another, and
2 intention permanently to deprive.

This reflects the intangible nature of services: they cannot belong to anyone because they have no physical presence.

Actus reus elements

Services

Theft Act 1978, s.1(2)

It is obtaining of services where the other is induced to confer a benefit by doing some act, or causing or permitting some act to be done, on the understanding that the benefit has been or will be paid for.

Problem area: benefit, value and payment

Confusion surrounds obtaining services by **deception** due to the common belief that the offence requires the defendant to act fraudulently in order to avoid making payment.

There is reference to payment in s.1(2) but this refers to the idea that there is some reciprocal exchange between the parties, i.e. there must be an agreement to provide X in return for Y (Y may be money but need not be).

For example, if Andrew agrees to build a bookcase (X) for Bethan if she washes his curtains (Y), there is an exchange of valuable services although there is no payment of money. If Andrew lied about the bookcase in order to get his curtains washed, he will be liable for obtaining services by deception.

This common error can be avoided if you look for the two essential elements in the problem: (1) deception leading to obtaining (2) services. This is illustrated by the examples below (only the first relates to payment):

■ Andrew pretends that he will pay Vinnie £10 (**deception**) for washing his car (service).

- Bethan is a disqualified driver. She uses her friend's licence (**deception**) to hire a car (service).
- Carol pretends to be a member of the National Trust (**deception**) in order to get free entry into a museum (service).
- Dan (14) lies about his age (**deception**) so that he can take part in a skydiving course that has a minimum age restriction (18) (service).

Obtaining a money transfer by deception

KEY STATUTORY PROVISION

Theft Act 1968, s.15A(1)

A person is guilty of an offence if, by any deception, he dishonestly obtains a money transfer for himself or another.

Two *actus reus* elements	Two *mens rea* elements
obtaining by deception	dishonesty
money transfer	intention/recklessness as to deception

Section 15A was enacted to avoid the implications of *Preddy*.

KEY CASE

R v. *Preddy* [1996] 3 All ER 481

Concerning: obtaining property by deception, mortgage fraud

Facts

The defendants made false representations about income, occupation and other factors in order to obtain mortgages. Payments were made by electronic transfer.

Legal principle

The convictions were quashed. In a money transfer, funds from the source account are extinguished and a credit balance is created in the destination account. The credit balance is a new *chose in action* that has never belonged to anyone else hence it cannot be 'property belonging to another' so it cannot give rise to liability under s.15.

This loophole was filled by the creation of a new offence, s.15A, which avoided the complicated issue of credit balances as property by concentrating on the movement of money between accounts.

Theft Act 1968, s.15A(2)

A money transfer occurs when –

(a) a debit is made from one account,
(b) a credit is made to another, and
(c) the credit results from the debit or the debit results from the credit.

Problem area: money, credit cards/cheques and credit balances

Problems involving deception offences frequently include consumer transactions. A successful answer will demonstrate understanding of the way that the various forms of payment give rise to liability. Remember that all forms of payment are treated differently by the law as to the way that they are understood in everyday society.

Money has value to people due to its purchasing capacity rather than its physical existence. If someone replaces your £50 note with five £10 notes, you will not mind because it has the same value. The law, however, is concerned with this unauthorised substitution of one piece of property (1 × £50) with another (5 × £10) rather than its value (£50 irrespective of its composition). To understand money from a legal perspective, swap money for cars: if someone takes your VW Golf and returns a Ford Fiesta (both worth £1000), you still have a car of the same value but you will object to the unauthorised substitution of different property. This is how the law regards money; by its physical existence not its value.

Credit cards and cheques should also be regarded in terms of their physical presence as pieces of plastic and paper *with no inherent value* that can be stolen (theft of physical property). If they are used, the owner's account reduces accordingly and this may be theft of a *thing in action* (credit balance) but the two should not be confused. Their use will also give rise to obtaining property/services by deception as the defendant represents that he is authorised to use the card.

Credit balances are *things in action* which means that a person can sue his bank to recover his money if it were withheld (hence it is a 'thing' that the account holder can bring an 'action' to recover). The use of a stolen cheque or credit card reduces the account holder's balance thus is theft of a *thing in action* as the money that can be recovered from the bank by legal action is reduced or eliminated.

Credit balances are the subject matter of the s.15A offence following the decision in *Preddy* that fraudulently-obtained mortgage transfers were not 'property belonging to another'. *Preddy* can be difficult to understand as we think of credit transfers as the transfer of property. If Adam transfers money from his account to Ben's, we think of this as Adam transferring *his property* to Ben. In law, this is not the case. Once Adam transfers his credit balance, he cannot recover it from his bank so it is extinguished. The new credit balance created in Ben's account has never belonged to Adam as he has never had the ability to sue to recover it from Ben's bank. This strange way of thinking about the transfer of money arises from the way that credit balances are viewed in law as *things in action* which cannot be transferred between accounts. This was why a new offence was needed to deal with credit transfers induced by deception.

■ Making off without payment

KEY STATUTORY PROVISION

Theft Act 1978, s.3

A person who, knowing that payment on the spot for any goods supplied or service done is required or expected from him, dishonestly makes off without having paid as required or expected and with intent to avoid payment of the amount due shall be guilty of an offence.

Three *actus reus* elements	Three *mens rea* elements
goods supplied/services done	dishonesty
making off from spot where payment is required/ expected	knowledge that payment on the spot was required/expected
without paying as required/expected	intention to avoid making payment

The key to understanding this offence and identifying it in a problem scenario is to think about why it exists.

Section 15 (TA 1968) and s.1 (TA 1978) require that deception occurs *before* property or services are obtained; a defendant who decides not to pay *after* obtaining property/services will not be liable. Therefore, a defendant who orders a meal intending to pay but changes his mind when presented with the bill would not incur liability. The offence of making off without payment catches this situation.

It often involves irretrievable property:

■ petrol: mingles with the petrol already in the tank and thus is impossible to return
■ restaurant food: cannot be returned after consumption

■ services: cannot be given back after they have been performed.

The elements of the offence are not complicated:

■ *Goods supplied/services provided.* Property/services retain the same meaning.
■ *Making off from the spot where payment is expected/required.* This is usually obvious. In *Aziz* [1993] Crim LR 708, this spot was held to be mobile in relation to taxi journeys rather than the defendant's stated or desired destination. Making off does not necessitate a dramatic exit or deliberate stealth; any departure will suffice (although speed or stealth may be evidence of a guilty state of mind).
■ *Without paying as required/expected.* Making off does not require a dramatic exit or deliberate stealth (although these are often evidence of wrongdoing). The defendant must make no offer of payment: an agreement to return later, even if not honest, defeats the offence (*Vincent* [2001] 1 WLR 1172).
■ *Dishonesty.* Uses the *Ghosh* test (Chapter 13).
■ *Knowledge that payment on the spot was required/expected.* This is closely linked with dishonesty. A defendant who thought, for example, that a friend would be paying the bill does not know that payment is required/expected thus may not be considered to be dishonest if he left without making payment.
■ *Intention to avoid payment.* Requires intention to avoid payment permanently. In *Allen* [1985] AC 1029, it was held that an intention to temporarily avoid payment will not suffice so a defendant who left a hotel owing a large bill which he genuinely hoped to be able to pay at a later date was not liable.

Chapter summary:
Putting it all together

TEST YOURSELF

- ☐ Can you tick all the points from the revision checklist at the beginning of this chapter?
- ☐ Take the **end-of-chapter quiz** on the companion website.
- ☐ Test your knowledge of the cases with the **revision flashcards** on the website.
- ☐ Attempt the problem question from the beginning of the chapter using the guidelines below.
- ☐ Go to the companion website to try out other questions.

Answer guidelines

See the problem question at the start of the chapter. A diagram illustrating how to structure your answer is available on the website.

Points to remember when answering this question

- There are three potential events that give rise to liability for David: (1) using the credit card to buy trainers, (2) using his brother's gym membership and (3) failing to pay for the meal. Discuss each of these separately before moving on to Delilah.
- Explain *why* you have chosen a particular offence as the basis for liability. This is particularly important if there is more than one offence raised by a particular set of facts as there is in relation to the purchase of the trainers.
- Work through the elements of each of the offences methodically. This chapter deals only with the elements that were not covered in Chapter 13 but remember to include all elements of the offence in your answer.

Make your answer really stand out

- Certain points are always trickier than others. Try to spot these and give them additional attention. This shows your examiner that you are able to (a) spot the complex issues and (b) deal with them effectively. Here, you might want to tackle (1) the dual liability created by use of the credit card and (2) liability for obtaining services by deception even though there was no payment involved.
- Although you must focus on answering the question rather than providing lengthy descriptions of the law, it can impress the examiner if you include some explanation of your analysis in the answer. Here, it would be useful to explain why David and Delilah are liable for different offences when what they have done is, in essence, the same.

16
Insanity and automatism

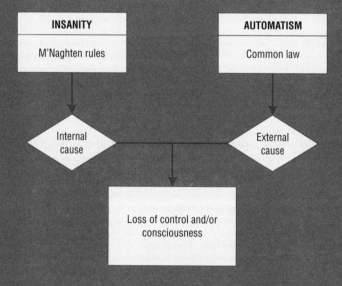

Revision checklist

What you need to know:

- [ ] M'Naghten rules to establish insanity
- [ ] Difference between medical and legal insanity
- [ ] Relationship between insanity and automatism
- [ ] Internal/external causes distinction

Introduction:
Understanding insanity and automatism

If a defendant is unable to control his movements or behaviour, his conduct is involuntary and should not lead to criminal liability.

Insanity and automatism both give rise to situations in which a person is unable to control his movement and/or behaviour. Insanity is caused by internal factors whilst automatism arises from external factors. Despite the obvious similarities between them, they have radically different outcomes for the defendant: automatism leads to acquittal whilst insanity results in a 'special verdict of ' not guilty by reason of insanity'. For this reason, an ability to identify and distinguish between them is essential.

Essay question advice

Essays on insanity tend to focus on its outdated nature and need for reform. Essay questions criticising the internal/external distinction are relatively common and involve both insanity and automatism.

Problem question advice

Insanity and automatism will combine with one (or more) offence(s), They could arise in relation to any offence but are frequently combined with homicide and non-fatal offences. Any lapse in consciousness or control should trigger a discussion of insanity (internal cause) or automatism (external cause).

Sample question

Could you answer this question? Below is a typical essay question that could arise on this topic. Guidelines on answering the question are included at the end of the chapter, whilst a sample problem question and guidance on tackling it can be found on the companion website.

Insanity has been described as a 'quagmire of law seldom entered into nowadays save by those in desperate need of some kind of defence'.

Explain and comment upon this view of insanity.

■ Insanity

KEY DEFINITION

Insanity At the time of committing the act, the defendant was labouring under such a defect of reason, arising from a defect of mind, that he did not know the nature and quality of his act or, if he did know this, that he did not know that what he was doing was wrong (*M'Naghten Rules* (1843) 10 Cl & Fin 200). See Figure 16.1.

Figure 16.1

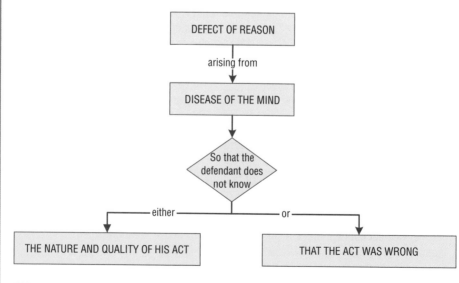

Apply the M'Naghten Rules to establish **insanity**. If the conclusion does not coincide with your perception of insanity, e.g. diabetes and epilespy, accept this as a consequence of judicial interpretation. Insanity is a label applied to those who are not responsible for their actions when the offence was committed; it will not necesssarily accord with medical or everyday ideas of insanity.

Defect of reason

A defect of reason arises when the defendant is incapable of exercising ordinary powers of reasoning.

KEY CASE

R v. *Clarke* [1972] 1 All ER 291

Concerning: defect of reason

Facts

The defendant was charged with theft after putting groceries in her bag. She claimed she acted absent-mindedly whilst suffering from depression. The trial judge ruled that this amounted to a defect of reason and raised **insanity**.

Legal principle

It was held that 'defect of reason' required inability to exercise reason rather than a failure to do so at a time at which the exercise of reason was possible. The defendant in this case failed to exercise powers of reason but was not incapable of reasoning thus was not within the scope of insanity.

Defect of reason requires an *inability* to reason, not *failure* to reason. Look for evidence of:

- ability to reason: rational thinking, controlled behaviour.
- inability to reason: irrationality, strange or abnormal thoughts/behaviour.

Disease of the mind

Judicial interpretation of disease of the mind has moved the legal definition far away from the medical conception of **insanity**.

R v. *Sullivan* [1984] AC 156

Concerning: disease of the mind

Facts

The defendant caused GBH during an epileptic fit.

Legal principle

The House of Lords held that the nature of the disease, physical or psychological, was irrelevant provided it affected the 'mental faculties of reason, memory and understanding' at the time of the offence.

This means that *any disease* that affects the way that the mind reasons, remembers or comprehends is a 'disease of the mind' for the purposes of insanity and demonstrates a distinction between:

■ disease of the mind (any disease that affects the functioning of the brain), and
■ disease of the brain (more akin to mental illness).

Problem area: internal and external causes

This approach to 'disease of the mind' creates potential for everyday physical conditions to amount to insanity. This is a particular problem in relation to the divide between **insanity** (internal cause) and automatism (external cause) as physical conditions will always amount to an internal factor and give rise to insanity. The implications of this are illustrated in relation to diabetes.

Internal cause: diabetics who fail to take medication (*hyper*glycaemia: high blood sugar) fall within insanity because the loss of consciousness/control arises from the disease itself (*Hennessy* [1989] 2 All ER 9).

External cause: diabetics who experience an adverse reaction to their medication (*hypo*glycaemia: low blood sugar) can rely on automatism as their inability to reason arises from an external cause, i.e. their medication (*Quick* [1973] QB 910). The exception to this occurs if the defendant was reckless in mismanaging his medication in which his automatism is regarded as self-induced thus cannot be relied upon to avoid liability (*Bailey* [1983] 2 All ER 503).

EXAM TIP

Examiners often use diabetes to test understanding of internal/external causes so it is worth making sure that you understand the distinction and relevant cases as well as ensuring accuracy with terminology in relation to *hyper* and *hypo*glycaemia.

Nature and quality of the act

This requires lack of awareness of the *physical* nature and quality of the act (not its moral qualities). There must be a difference between the defendant's action and what he thinks he is doing:

- The *nature* of the act concerns its *characteristics*, e.g. the defendant put a baby on the fire believing it was a log.
- The *quality* of the act concerns its *consequences*, e.g. the defendant cut off the sleeping victim's head in order to watch him looking for it in the morning; he was aware of the nature of decapitation but not of its consequences.
- *Delusional motives* will not suffice, e.g. a defendant who battered his wife to death to prevent her abduction by aliens remains aware of the nature and quality of his act.

Knowledge that the act is wrong

If the defendant is aware of the nature and quality of his act, he may still raise insanity in his defence if he does not know that his actions are wrong (legally rather than morally).

KEY CASE

R v. *Windle* [1952] 2 QB 826

Concerning: knowledge an act is legally wrong

Facts

The defendant was medically insane. He gave his suicidal wife an overdose. Upon arrest, he made reference to the likelihood he would hang for his actions.

Legal principle

'Wrong' means 'contrary to law'. The defendant's comment showed awareness that his conduct was contrary to law so insanity was not established. It was irrelevant that he believed he was morally justified or that society in general would not condemn his actions.

Questions have been raised about conflict between the M'Naghten Rules and Article 5 of the European Convention on Human Rights which protects against the arbitrary deprivation of liberty, although it contains an exception in relation to 'unsound mind'. It was held in *Winterwerp* v. *Netherlands* (1979) 2 EHRR 387 that a person should only be detained on the basis of 'unsound mind' if three criteria were satisfied:

1 There is a strong correlation between legal and medical definitions of insanity
2 The court's decision that the defendant is of unsound mind is based on objective medical evidence.
3 The court believes that the mental disorder is one that necessitates compulsory confinement.

Clearly, there are inconsistencies with this approach and the M'Naghten Rules. Prepare for an essay on this topic by reading: Mackay, R.D. and Gearty, C.A., 'On Being Insane in Jersey' [2001] *Criminal Law Review* 560.

■Automatism

Automatism An act which is done by the muscles without any control by the mind such as a spasm, a reflex action, or a convulsion; or an act done by a person who is not conscious of what he is doing such as an act done whilst suffering from concussion: *Bratty* v. *Attorney-General for NI* [1963] AC 386.

There are three requirements of automatism:

1 complete loss of control
2 an external cause
3 automatism must not be self-induced.

Complete loss of control

As automatism is based on involuntary actions, the defendant must suffer complete loss of control and/or consciousness rather than an eroded ability to exercise control or partially impaired consciousness.

Broome v. *Perkins* [1987] Crim LR 271

Concerning: loss of control

Facts

The defendant sought to rely on automatism for charges arising from erratic driving whilst in hypoglycaemic shock.

Legal principle

Automatism requires a complete loss of control. The defendant maintained *some* control by steering and braking thus his movements were not entirely involuntary and automatism would not be available.

External cause

The distinction between automatism and insanity is based upon external and internal causes of loss of control. External causes such as blows to the head or the introduction of medication into the defendant's system thus give rise to automatism.

Automatism must not be self-induced

Automatism leads to acquittal in recognition that the defendant's inability to control his actions render him blameless for this behaviour. It follows that self-induced automatism cannot be used to avoid liability because the defendant was responsible for his lack of control:

■ In *Bailey* (above) failing to eat after taking insulin despite awareness that this could lead to uncontrolled behaviour amounted to self-induced automatism.
■ Disassociative states caused by consumption of alcohol or non-prescription drugs amount to self-induced automatism.

EXAM TIP

Although cases on self-induced automatism have only arisen in relation to diabetes, the principle is generally applicable. Remember this if you encounter a problem question where a defendant suffers an adverse reaction to taking too much medication or from combining alcohol and medication, for example, irrespective of the ailment for which the medication is prescribed. Adding a sentence that explains that this is analogous to the situation concerning the mismanagement of insulin by diabetics will really help your answer stand out.

Chapter summary:
Putting it all together

☐ Can you tick all the points from the revision checklist at the beginning of this chapter?

☐ Take the **end-of-chapter quiz** on the companion website.

☐ Test your knowledge of the cases with the **revision flashcards** on the website.

☐ Attempt the essay question from the beginning of the chapter using the guidelines below.

☐ Go to the companion website to try out other questions.

Answer guidelines

See the essay question at the start of the chapter. A diagram illustrating how to structure your answer is available on the website.

Points to remember when answering this question

▪ Descriptive answers that do not address the issue(s) raised in the question attract little credit so be sure to work out exactly what the question requires, i.e. do not just write everything you can think of about insanity.

▪ Work out what the question requires by rephrasing in simple terms, e.g. 'the law on insanity is confused and defendants are reluctant to rely on it'. This leads you to two key issues that need to be addressed (1) what is wrong with the law and (2) why is it used infrequently by defendants.

▪ Make sure that you know enough about a topic before attempting a question on it. Here, the minimum requirement would be an ability to state and explain the M'Naghten Rules and to identify and criticise relevant cases as well as comment on why defendants are reluctant to rely on insanity (stigma, disposal).

Make your answer really stand out

▪ Can you identify the source of the quotation? If so, do it at the start of your answer to make a real impact with the examiner. It can also point you towards relevant discussion: 'this quotation is from *Quick* which raises the internal/external issue'.

▪ Demonstrate an awareness of the problems caused by the divergence between legal and medical/social definitions of insanity, particularly with reference to the stigma associated with medical insanity that causes defendants to plead guilty rather than rely on insanity.

▪ An ability to incorporate references to Article 5 ECHR will impress your examiners.

17
Intoxication

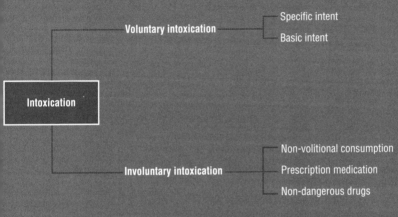

Revision checklist

What you need to know:

- ☐ Distinction between voluntary and involuntary intoxication
- ☐ Meaning of basic and specific intent and the relevance to intoxication
- ☐ Clash of policy and principle in relation to intoxication

Introduction:
Understanding intoxication

'I only did it because I was drunk' is a frequently-expressed sentiment which is accepted as an excuse for all sorts of bad behaviour.

This is because it is well-established that alcohol and drugs alter people's behaviour and attitudes. It is also true that a great deal of crime, particularly involving violence, is committed whilst the defendant is intoxicated. How, then, does the law view intoxication? It is essential that you understand the issues that have led to the development of a dual set of rules – voluntary and involuntary intoxication – as the courts attempt to reconcile principle and policy in relation to the intoxicated defendant.

Essay question advice

Essay questions will either focus solely on intoxication or include it within a question about states of mind generally (Chapter 3). Aim to locate your discussion in the context of the principle/policy debate as this is a tricky point and one that is often overlooked.

Problem question advice

Problems frequently include intoxicated victims and the level of detail required on intoxication can vary enormously. A simple issue may require a single sentence explaining that voluntary intoxication is not a defence to crimes of basic intent whilst a more complex situation could combine intoxication with defences or raise issues of involuntary intoxication. The final complication is that intoxication could arise in relation to any offence so it really could pop up in absolutely any problem question. Remember that intoxication covers prescription drugs as well as alcohol and recreational drugs.

Sample question

Could you answer this question? Below is a typical problem question that could arise on this topic. Guidelines on answering the question are included at the end of the chapter, whilst a sample essay question and guidance on tackling it can be found on the companion website.

Problem question

Douglas suspects that his wife, Valerie, is having an affair with Derek. After several hours of heavy drinking, he decides to confront her at Derek's house. Douglas storms into the house and finds Valerie lying naked on the floor. Enraged, he attacks her with a nearby poker, inflicting serious injuries. The noise rouses Derek from his drug-induced stupor. The effects of the hallucinogenic drugs that he has taken lead him to conclude that Douglas is an alien so he swings a knife at him, severing his hand. It later transpired that Valerie had given Derek the drugs earlier in the evening, telling him they were headache tablets.

Discuss the impact of intoxication on the liabilty of Douglas and Derek.

■ Types of intoxication

Intoxication may be voluntary or involuntary:

Figure 17.1

VOLUNTARY INTOXICATION	INVOLUNTARY INTOXICATION
The defendant has knowingly ingested recreational drugs or alcohol, knowing their nature. This includes situations where the defendant has knowingly consumed alcohol but is mistaken as to its strength or where he has knowingly taken recreational drugs but is unclear about the effect they will have on him.	The defendant is unaware that he has ingested drugs or alcohol. It also covers intentional consumption of non-dangerous drugs (in accordance with instructions) or drugs such as valium that are known to have a soporific effect (provided the defendant was not reckless in taking them).
The defendant is to blame for his inability to control his behaviour so should not avoid liability for his actions unless he is so intoxicated that he is incapable of thought or reason.	The defendant is not to blame for his intoxication so should not be held reasonable for the consequences of it.

Voluntary intoxication

Although intoxication is viewed as something which affects behaviour, in law the emphasis is on its impact on the defendant's mind, specifically his ability to form *mens rea*. It is only if the defendant is so intoxicated that his ability to form *mens rea* is impaired that the law may take account of his voluntary intoxication. The extent to which it does so depends upon the nature of the offence he has committed as a distinction is made between crimes of specific and basic intent.

Specific and basic intent

The most straightforward way to distinguish crimes of specific and basic intent is based on the *mens rea* of the offence (see Figure 17.2).

Figure 17.2

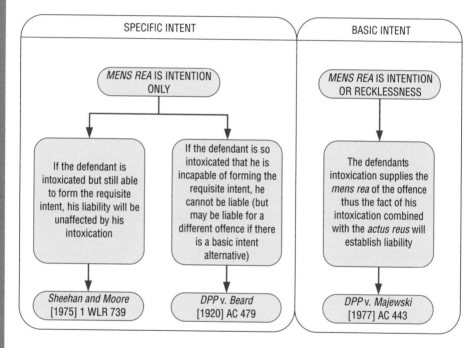

- This illustrates that the level of the defendant's intoxication is central to determining how his liability will be affected.
- The exception to this rule relates to *Dutch courage* situations, which are outlined in Figure 17.3:

Figure 17.3

CHAIN OF EVENTS	A-G for Northern Ireland v. Gallagher [1963] AC 349
The defendant forms the intention to commit a specific intent offence.	The defendant decides to kill his wife.
He consumes quantities of alcohol to give himself the courage to commit the *actus reus* of the offence.	He buys a knife and a bottle of whiskey, which he drinks to give himself the courage to go through with the killing.
He commits the *actus reus* whilst in a state of intoxication which is such that he lacks *mens rea*.	Whilst intoxicated, he cuts his wife's throat.
Should he be able to rely upon his intoxication to avoid liability?	He argued that he was so intoxicated that he was incapable of forming the intention to kill at the time he killed his wife.

KEY CASE

A-G for Northern Ireland v. *Gallagher* [1963] AC 349

Concerning: Dutch courage

Facts

See Figure 17.3.

Legal principle

It was held that a person who forms an intention to kill whilst sober and drinks to give himself Dutch courage to do the killing and who then goes on to kill whilst intoxicated cannot rely on intoxication to avoid liability.

FURTHER THINKING

According to principle, *actus reus* and *mens rea* must coincide. Application of this principle would result in acquittal in Dutch courage cases as the defendant would not be able to form *mens rea* due to his intoxication.

Policy has prevailed here as a person who forms *mens rea* and negates that with intoxication in order to commit the offence is nonetheless held liable. As Lord Denning said 'the wickedness of his mind before he got drunk is enough to condemn him, coupled with the act which he intended and did do'.

Basic intent

Policy considerations are evident in relation to voluntary intoxication and basic intent. A defendant cannot argue that he failed to recognise a risk of harm because he was intoxicated. The House of Lords in *Majewski* extended this further.

KEY CASE

DPP v. *Majewski* [1977] AC 443

Concerning: basic intent, intoxication

Facts

The defendant attacked a police-officer whilst voluntarily intoxicated. He argued that he was so intoxicated that he could not form the requisite *mens rea*.

Legal principle

The effect of intoxication on the defendant's state of mind was only relevant to crimes of specific intent. In crimes of basic intent, the defendant's recklessness in taking drugs that rendered his behaviour uncontrolled and unpredictable was in itself sufficient to substitute for the *mens rea* of the offence.

In other words, if the *mens rea* of the offence includes recklessness, this is satisfied by the defendant's intoxication because it is reckless to render oneself into a state where behaviour cannot be controlled and crimes may be committed.

FURTHER THINKING

Majewski is open to criticism because it replaces the *mens rea* of an offence with abstract recklessness associated with becoming intoxicated. This means that all drunken people are walking around with the *mens rea* of all basic intent offences that will lead to liability if they happen to commit the *actus reus* whilst drunk!

Essays may invite critical analysis of this position. The following article provides in-depth discussion of the implications of *Majewski* so would be excellent preparation for an essay: Gardner, S., 'The Importance of *Majewski*' [1984] OJLS 279.

You could also gain credit by commenting on proposals for reform of the law on intoxication. Virgo's article provides a useful summary of Law Commission proposals and a critique of their effectiveness: Virgo, G., 'The Law Commission Consultation Paper on Intoxication and Criminal Liability Reconciling Principle and Policy' [1993] *Criminal Law Review* 415.

Involuntary intoxication

Involuntary intoxication falls into three categories.

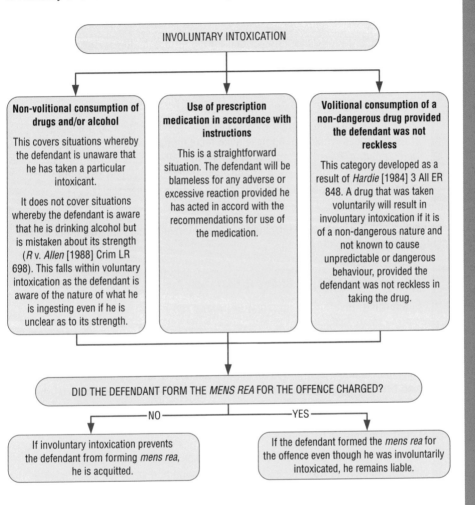

INVOLUNTARY INTOXICATION

Non-volitional consumption of drugs and/or alcohol

This covers situations whereby the defendant is unaware that he has taken a particular intoxicant.

It does not cover situations whereby the defendant is aware that he is drinking alcohol but is mistaken about its strength (*R* v. *Allen* [1988] Crim LR 698). This falls within voluntary intoxication as the defendant is aware of the nature of what he is ingesting even if he is unclear as to its strength.

Use of prescription medication in accordance with instructions

This is a straightforward situation. The defendant will be blameless for any adverse or excessive reaction provided he has acted in accord with the recommendations for use of the medication.

Volitional consumption of a non-dangerous drug provided the defendant was not reckless

This category developed as a result of *Hardie* [1984] 3 All ER 848. A drug that was taken voluntarily will result in involuntary intoxication if it is of a non-dangerous nature and not known to cause unpredictable or dangerous behaviour, provided the defendant was not reckless in taking the drug.

DID THE DEFENDANT FORM THE *MENS REA* FOR THE OFFENCE CHARGED?

— NO —   —YES—

If involuntary intoxication prevents the defendant from forming *mens rea*, he is acquitted.

If the defendant formed the *mens rea* for the offence even though he was involuntarily intoxicated, he remains liable.

R v. *Hardie* [1985] 1 WLR 64

Concerning: involuntary intoxication, non-dangerous drugs

Facts

The defendant took valium prescribed for his girlfriend after an argument, believing it would calm him down. Under its influence, he started a fire which spread through the flat.

Legal principle

This did not fall within voluntary intoxication thus the *Majewski* presumption of recklessness would not apply. Unlike recreational drugs and alcohol, which were known to cause unpredictable behaviour, valium was known for its sedative effects. Consumption of non-dangerous drugs would amount to involuntary intoxication unless the consumption itself was reckless.

The way in which liability is determined in cases of involuntary intoxication is further demonstrated by *Kingston*.

R v. *Kingston* (1994) 99 Cr App R 286

Concerning: involuntary intoxication, *mens rea*

Facts

The defendant was drugged without his knowledge by men who wished to blackmail him and committed an act of indecency with a young boy who had also been drugged. He claimed that the drugs eroded his ability to resist the paedophilic urges that he managed to control whilst sober.

Legal principle

Although the defendant's will was weakened by drugs administered without his knowledge, he was still aware of his situation and knew his actions were wrong. As such, he had *mens rea* for the offence charged.

Therefore, involuntary intoxication only absolves the defendant of liability if it renders him incapable of forming *mens rea*, not if it caused him to commit an offence he would not have committed if sober.

Chapter summary:
Putting it all together

☐ Can you tick all the points from the revision checklist at the beginning of this chapter?

☐ Take the **end-of-chapter quiz** on the companion website.

☐ Test your knowledge of the cases with the **revision flashcards** on the website.

☐ Attempt the problem question from the beginning of the chapter using the guidelines below.

☐ Go to the companion website to try out other questions.

Answer guidelines

See the problem question at the start of the chapter. A diagram illustrating how to structure your answer is available on the website.

Points to remember when answering this question

■ There are multiple parties so untangle the facts to determine what each party has done and structure your answer around this.

■ The question involves intoxication and non-fatal offences so you would need to be confident on both topics to tackle this question. It is a popular combination as non-fatal offences divide in terms of specific (s.18) and basic (s.20) intent.

■ Establish liability for an offence before discussing the ability of a defence even though the question focuses attention on intoxication.

■ Use the diagrams in this chapter to determine whether each situation involves voluntary or involuntary intoxication.

■ If intoxication is voluntary, remember the law treats crimes of basic and specific intent differently.

Make your answer really stand out

■ Make effective use of key cases to support your argument. The *Majewksi* principle is frequently omitted because it is hard to understand so make sure that you can include this case and use it effectively.

18
Self-defence

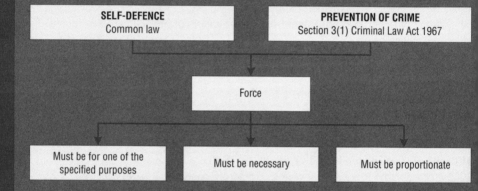

Revision checklist

What you need to know:

- [ ] Relationship between self-defence and prevention of crime
- [ ] Situations in which it is lawful to use force
- [ ] Impact of mistaken belief on the necessity to use force
- [ ] Determination of level of force that is appropriate

Introduction:
Understanding self-defence

There are circumstances in which force, even fatal force, used against another is justified and will not give rise to criminal liability.

A person can use force to protect himself, his property and other people against threats of harm. Force may also be used to prevent the commission of a crime or to apprehend an offender.

The range of circumstances in which it is lawful to use force demonstrates the breadth of self-defence. Although usually described as a defence, self-defence is actually the absence of the unlawfulness element of the *actus reus* of fatal and non-fatal offences. As force used in self-defence is regarded as *lawful*, this unlawfulness requirement is not satisfied.

The operation of self-defence has been quite controversial so it is important to take account of principles in the area and the policy behind them in understanding this topic.

Essay question advice

Self-defence can be a contentious area, particularly following the high-profile case of Tony Martin (*Martin (Anthony)* [2003] QB 1) and the subsequent debate over the position of householders who attack intruders in their homes which has led to the Criminal Law (Amendment) (Protection of Property) Bill 2005. This makes it a potential topic for critical evaluation in an essay question.

Problem question advice

Issues of self-defence are generally raised in relation to fatal and non-fatal offences against the person. Look out for facts that suggest that the defendant's conduct was prompted by fears of attack (on himself, others or property) or that he was acting to prevent a crime.

Sample question

Could you answer this question? Below is a typical problem question that could arise on this topic. Guidelines on answering the question are included at the end of the chapter, whilst a sample essay question and guidance on tackling it can be found on the companion website.

Problem question

Vernon makes advances to Davina at a party. Undeterred by her refusal, he follows her into a bedroom and pushes her onto the bed. Afraid he is going to rape her, Davina pushes him hard causing him to fall off the bed and he breaks his arm. Davina rushes towards the door but then returns and kicks Vernon hard in the groin, causing bruising.

Davina tells Donald what has happened. He sees a man with a broken arm who he thinks is Vernon (but who is actually Victor) so he tackles him to the ground, shouting, 'He's a rapist, call the police.'

Discuss Davina and Donald's liability.

■ Scope of self-defence

Self-defence is convenient shorthand for two separate (but similar) situations that negate the unlawfulness of otherwise unlawful acts (see Figure 18.1).

Figure 18.1

Self-defence	Prevention of crime
It is both good law and good sense that a man who is attacked may defend himself. It is both good law and good sense that he may do, but only do, what is reasonably necessary' (*Palmer* v. *R* [1971] AC 814).	'A person may use such force as is reasonable in the circumstances in the prevention of crime, or in effecting or assisting in the lawful arrest of offenders or suspected offenders or of persons unlawfully at large' (s. 3(1) Criminal Law Act 1967)

POTENTIAL OVERLAP
A man who shoots a person who is attacking him both acts to defend himself and to prevent a crime.

The operation of common law and statute justifies the use of force in the following situations:

- **Protection of oneself:** Sam runs towards Derek waving a samurai sword. Derek throws a rock at him to stop his charge which hits Sam on the head and kills him.
- **Protection of another person:** Derek sees Sam holding down a woman and believing that Sam is raping her, Derek smashes him over the head with his umbrella, knocking him unconscious.
- **Protection of property:** Derek sees Sam pick up a rock and moves towards Derek's car. Believing that Sam is going to smash the window, Derek rugby tackles him to the ground, breaking his wrist.
- **Prevention of crime:** Derek sees Sam following an elderly lady and suspects he is going to steal her bag. Derek picks up a fallen tree branch and runs at Sam brandishing it. The branch causes scratches to Sam's retinas and seriously damages his sight.
- **Apprehension of an offender or person unlawfully at large:** Derek is having coffee when he hears shouts of 'stop thief'. He looks up to see Sam running towards him carrying a lady's handbag with two policemen in pursuit. He sticks out his leg which Sam falls over and breaks both wrists in the fall.

■ Elements of self-defence

The situations outlined above justify the use of force but there are limitations as to the level of force that may be used. Self-defence must involve 'reasonable force'. This has two elements (see Figure 18.2).

Figure 18.2

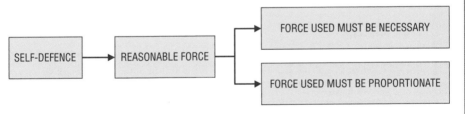

Necessity of force

Self-defence justifies the use of force that would otherwise be unlawful. In order to be justified, it must be necessary for the defendant to have used force.

Three questions are relevant in determining whether it was necessary for the defendant to use force:

- Is it necessary to use force if the defendant has an opportunity to retreat?

- Does the defendant have to wait to be attacked before the use of force is necessary?
- Is self-defence available to a defendant who is mistaken about the necessity of using force?

Duty to retreat

Failing to take advantage of an opportunity to retreat may make it difficult for the defendant to argue that the use of force was necessary. In *Bird* [1985] 2 All ER 513, it was said that attempts to retreat indicate an unwillingness to fight so may negate any suggestion of retaliation or revenge.

EXAM TIP

If the defendant had the opportunity to retreat but did not do so, it is not fatal to reliance on self-defence, but you will need to use the facts available to demonstrate that the defendant was not eager for a fight or that it was reasonable in the circumstances for him to stand his ground.

Pre-emptive force

KEY CASE

Beckford v. *R* [1988] AC 130

Concerning: pre-emptive attack

Facts

The defendant, a police officer, shot and killed an armed man who had been threatening others with a gun.

Legal principle

Lord Griffiths stated that 'a man about to be attacked does not have to wait for his assailant to strike the first blow or fire the first shot; circumstances may justify a pre-emptive strike'.

Not only may a person resort to force in order to prevent an anticipated attack, it has been held that he may arm himself in order to do so. This has included making and storing fire bombs to protect property against attack from rioters: *Attorney-General's Reference (No 2 of 1983)* [1984] QB 456.

Mistake

A defendant who is mistaken about the need to use force has effectively attacked an innocent person. Although it could seem that self-defence should not be available in cases of mistaken belief, the courts have taken a different view.

R v. Williams (Gladstone) (1984) 78 Cr App R 276

Concerning: mistaken belief

Facts

The defendant observed one man attack another. He intervened and punched the attacker in order to protect the victim. However, the attacker had been trying to detain a man who had just committed a robbery so the defendant was charged as a result of his actions and sought to rely on self-defence.

Legal principle

The reasonableness of the defendant's actions must be judged on the facts as he believed them to be. If the defendant's perception of events had been correct, self-defence would have been available and he should not be deprived of a defence because he was mistaken. Provided the mistaken belief was honestly held, it is immaterial that the mistake was not reasonable.

EXAM TIP

This point often causes confusion, perhaps because it seems illogical to place such reliance on the defendant's impression of events. Remember that the question to be asked in relation to mistake is:

If the facts were as the defendant believed them to be, was the use of force necessary?

If the answer is 'yes' then the defendant may rely on self-defence even though it was not actually necessary, even if the mistake was not one that others would have made.

The law accommodates mistaken belief in self-defence as an acknowledgement that instant decisions made in stressful situations may be inaccurate. There are two situations in which the availability of mistaken belief is limited:

1 Where the mistake is made due to mental illness that has led the defendant to dramatically misinterpret events: *Martin (Anthony)* [2003] QB 1.
2 Where the mistake results from consumption of drugs or alcohol: *O'Grady* [1987] 3 All ER 420.

Level of force

Once it is established that the use of force was necessary, the next issue is to determine whether the level of force used was reasonable.

The general rule is that the force used must be *no more than necessary*; it must be proportionate to the threat. This means that the reasonableness of the force will depend upon the circumstances.

Although it is the defendant who determines whether the use of force is necessary, the reasonableness of the level of force is determined objectively, i.e. by the jury. Two factors must be taken into account:

1 The level of force must be reasonable in response to the facts as the defendant believed them to be: *Owino* [1996] 2 Cr App R 128.
2 Extreme situations can create pressure that distorts judgement: 'a person defending himself cannot weigh to a nicety the exact measure of his necessary defensive actions' (*Palmer* [1971] AC 814).

FURTHER THINKING

There is tension here between the emphasis on the defendant's interpretation of events in relation to the *necessity* to resort to force and the objective evaluation of the *level* of force. However, an objective element is a necessary safeguard against the use of excessive force in society.

For an excellent exposition of this issue in relation to force used against intruders, see Jefferson, M., 'Householders and the Use of Force against Intruders' J Crim Law (2005) vol. 69 pp. 405–415. This detailed article explains some complex points with clarity and would be useful reading prior to writing an essay on the topic.

■ Effect of self-defence

Self-defence justifies the force used so results in an outright acquittal if used successfully. There is no 'half-way measure' if, for example, the use of force was necessary but the level of force used was excessive: *Clegg* [1995] 1 All ER 334).

Chapter summary:
Putting it all together

☐ Can you tick all the points from the revision checklist at the beginning of this chapter?

☐ Take the **end-of-chapter quiz** on the companion website.

☐ Test your knowledge of the cases with the **revision flashcards** on the website.

☐ Attempt the problem question from the beginning of the chapter using the guidelines below.

☐ Go to the companion website to try out other questions.

Answer guidelines

See the problem question at the start of the chapter. A diagram illustrating how to structure your answer is available on the website.

Points to remember when answering this question

■ Although the question focuses on self-defence, the first step must always be to establish liability for an offence; if the defendant is not liable, he does not need a defence.

■ The offences here are non-fatal offences. These often arise with self-defence so make a good combination of revision topics.

■ There are two possible points of liability for Davina. Discuss these separately: they involve different levels of harm thus different offences (broken leg/s.20 OAPA; bruising/battery) and differ in the way that self-defence will operate.

■ Be logical in dealing with the elements of self-defence. Following the structure of the diagrams provided should ensure that you do not miss any key issues.

Make your answer really stand out

■ Remember that self-defence includes the s.3 CLA situations so look out for force used in the prevention of crime or apprehension of offenders. You could raise this point in relation to Davina to demonstrate your awareness of the overlap as she has both acted in her own defence and to prevent an offence (rape). It is also applicable to Donald who is acting to apprehend an offender.

■ Mistaken belief in the need to use force is a complex point and one that is often omitted or dealt with badly. Address this in relation to Donald; a careful application of *Williams (Gladstone)* should ensure that you reach an appropriate conclusion.

19
Duress

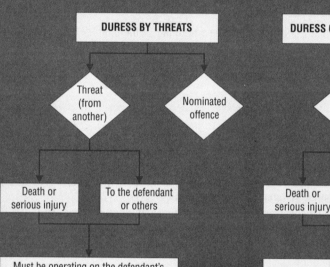

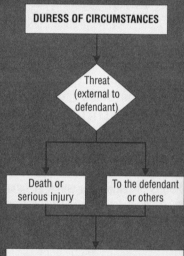

DURESS BY THREATS

Threat (from another)

Nominated offence

Death or serious injury

To the defendant or others

Must be operating on the defendant's mind at the time of the offence so that his will to resist is neutralised and he feels he has no option other than to commit the nominated offence.

DURESS OF CIRCUMSTANCES

Threat (external to defendant)

Death or serious injury

To the defendant or others

Must be operating on the defendant's mind at the time of the offence so that he feels he has no option other than to commit an offence.

Revision checklist

What you need to know:

- [ ] Operation of duress by threats and duress of circumstances
- [ ] Availability of the defences and the rationale for their operation
- [ ] Types of threat that suffice to establish duress
- [ ] Circumstances that remove the defence of duress from the defendant

Introduction:
Duress

Traditionally, duress could be described as a 'he made me do it' defence.

It was this aspect of compulsion that led to offences committed under duress being regarded as 'morally involuntary a s the defendant acts out of fear rather than choice. Duress of circumstances evolved as a second species of duress (with the former becoming known as 'duress by threats') because there were a broader range of situations in which the defendant seemed to act because he had no choice but which fell outside of duress by threats. This resulted in two closely related defences with many similar elements.

Essay question advice

Duress has attracted a fair amount of criticism based both on its existence as a defence and in terms of its operation so is a good topic for an essay. Either type of essay requires a detailed awareness of the operation of duress (both forms) and the rationale for its existence. Other areas could involve a comparison with self-defence (another absolute defence) or provocation (a similar two-stage test).

Problem question advice

General defences can combine with any offence so make sure that liability is established before defences are discussed. Look out for threats or other circumstances that make a defendant feel compelled to offend as evidence that duress is raised.

Sample question

Could you answer this question? Below is a typical problem question that could arise on this topic. Guidelines on answering the question are included at the end of the chapter, whilst a sample essay question and guidance on tackling it can be found on the companion website.

Debbie is involved with a group of older girls and has started experimenting with drugs and truanting from school. Jenny tells Debbie that unless she goes shoplifting with her, she will tell her mother about her drug-taking. Debbie reluctantly agrees and the girls steal from several shops. Jenny tells Debbie to steal a mobile phone from a girl in the park. Debbie refuses so Jenny produces a knife and threatens to scar her, so Debbie steals the phone. Debbie's brother, John, threatens to beat Debbie unless she burgles the home of an elderly neighbour who keeps his savings under his bed. Debbie initially refuses, eventually gives in but then cannot find the money.

Discuss Debbie's liability for property offences including any defences available to her.

■ Duress by threats

Duress is an absolute defence which leads to an acquittal. It is based on the notion that the defendant's will was overpowered by threats of harm to himself or others so that he had no choice other than to offend.

Nature of threat

Only threats of death or serious physical injury to the defendant (or certain others) will suffice. Threats of lesser harm, to damage property or reveal unpleasant or personal information, will not provide a basis for duress (even if they had an overwhelming influence on the defendant).

Immediacy

The requirement that the threat be immediate related to the notion that duress provided an inescapable pressure to offend but this has been broadened by judicial interpretation.

KEY CASE

R v. *Hudson and Taylor* [1971] 2 QB 202

Concerning: immediacy of threat

Facts

The defendants refused to give evidence at a trial because they had been threatened with violence if they did so by someone who was present in the courtroom. They gave false evidence which led to the acquittal of the accused and sought to rely on duress at their own trial for perjury. They were initially unsuccessful as it was held that the threats could not be carried out immediately.

Legal principle

The issue was not whether the threats could be carried out immediately but whether they were operating on the defendants at the time of the threat. The Court of Appeal recognised that threats were no less powerful because they were not immediately effective.

EXAM TIP

A threat which cannot be carried out at the time suggests an opportunity to avoid the threat which would negate any claim of duress. Following *Hudson and Taylor*, it is important to consider whether the threat was operating on the defendant's mind at the time that he committed the offence, notwithstanding the fact that the threat could not be carried out immediately.

Causal nexus

There must be a link between the threat made and the offence committed. Effectively, the person issuing the threat must nominate a particular offence to be committed.

KEY CASE

R v. *Cole* [1994] Crim LR 582

Concerning: nexus between threat and offence

Facts

The defendant was threatened with violence if he did not repay money that he owed. In desperation, he committed two armed robberies to make the repayments.

Legal principle

Duress was not available as those making the threats had not told the defendant to commit robbery. The decision to offend was the result of free choice by the defendant which was inconsistent with the defence of duress.

This is an important limitation on the availability of duress. In *Cole*, the lenders knew the defendant had exhausted all lawful means of obtaining money so must have realised that their threats would compel him to offend but their failure to specify an offence meant duress was not available.

This means that duress requires 'do *this* or else' rather than 'do *something* or else'.

Test for duress

R v. Howe [1987] 1 AC 417

Concerning: two-stage test

Facts

The defendant sought to rely on duress as a defence to murder on the basis that he believed that he would be killed if he did not kill the victim as instructed.

Legal principle

The House of Lords upheld the two-stage test outlined in *Graham* (1982) 74 Cr App R 235.

Figure 19.1

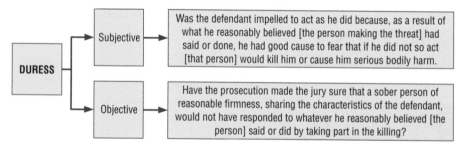

This two-stage test (see Figure 19.1) requires not only that the defendant *was* overwhelmed by threats but also that a sober person of reasonable firmness *would have been* compelled to offend. An objective angle limits the availability of duress by establishing a standard of fortitude expected of members of society. In other words, if an ordinary person in the defendant's position would have resisted the threats, the defendant's defence of duress will fail.

The Court of Appeal in *Bowen* [1996] 2 Cr App R 157 outlined three principles relevant to the attribution of the characteristics of the defendant to the reasonable man (see Figure 19.2).

Figure 19.2

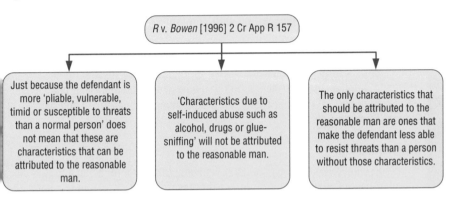

The characteristics that were thought to be relevant were:

- age
- sex
- pregnancy
- serious physical disability
- recognised mental illness/psychiatric conditions.

You might find it useful to compare the approach taken to the two-stage subjective-objective test in duress with that taken in provocation (Chapter 7), particularly with regards to the characteristics attributed to the reasonable man.

Availability of duress by threats

There are two factors that render duress unavailable:

1 voluntary association with a criminal gang
2 commission of murder or attempted murder.

Voluntary association with criminal organisations

Just as duress is denied to a defendant who did not take a reasonable opportunity to escape, it is also withheld from a defendant who put himself in a position where he might be pressurised into offending.

KEY CASE

R v. Sharp [1987] 1 QB 853

Concerning: voluntary association with criminals

Facts

The defendant took part in several armed robberies. When he tried to leave the gang, another member held a gun to his head and threatened to blow it off. He took part in a further robbery in which someone was killed and he sought to rely on duress.

Legal principle

A person who voluntarily joins a gang, knowing of its nature, as an active member cannot avail himself of duress if pressure is put upon him to offend.

Case law has elaborated on this principle:

- Gang membership does not always remove duress; it depends on the nature of the gang and the sort of activities in which it engages. A defendant should not expect violence from a non-violent gang: *Shepherd* (1988) 86 Cr App R 47.
- Membership of an organised gang is not essential. It is enough that the defendant puts himself in the position where he will encounter criminals with a tendency to violence, e.g. by buying drugs from a dealer: *Hasan* [2005] 2 AC 467.

Duress and murder

Duress is not a defence to murder. Its basis is that a defendant commits an offence as 'the lesser of two evils' in comparison with the harm with which he has been threatened. As murder involves taking a life, there can be no greater harm. The House of Lords in *Howe* stated that an ordinary man would rather sacrifice his own life than take the life of another. This principle was extended to attempted murder in *Gotts* [1992] 2 WLR 284.

FURTHER THINKING

Do you agree with *Howe*? Would an ordinary person sacrifice his life (or that of a loved one) to save the life of another, who might be unknown to him? How should this principle operate if the threat is to kill five people (or 15 or 50) if the life of one person is not taken? How does this rule stand when you consider that self-defence is available to murder (Chapter 18)? These complex questions are addressed in the following article which could be used to prepare for an essay on this topic: Elliot, D.W., 'Necessity, Duress and Self-Defence' [1989] *Criminal Law Review* 611.

Duress of circumstances

Duress of circumstances evolved as a species of duress by threats, initially in relation to motoring offences. It differs from duress by threats in two ways:

1 The threat does not have to come from another person. It may come from the surrounding circumstances or from a naturally occurring event.
2 The offence is not nominated by another. The defendant commits an offence not because he is ordered to do so by another but because it seems to be the only way of avoiding the threat that he faces.

KEY CASE

R v. *Willer* (1986) 83 Cr App R 225

Concerning: duress of circumstances

Facts
The defendant was the driver of a car which was being chased by a gang of youths who were threatening to kill him and his passenger. In order to escape them, the defendant drove through a pedestrian precinct.

Legal principle
It was held that the defendant should have a defence as he was 'wholly driven by the force of circumstances into doing what he did and did not drive the car otherwise than under that form of compulsion, i.e. under duress.

The principles relating to duress of circumstances have evolved through a series of cases. The following are the key points to remember:

- **The defendant's actions must be a reasonable and proportionate response to a threat of death or serious injury**. In *Martin* [1989] 1 All ER 652 the defendant's wife threatened to commit suicide unless he drove their son to work. This provided a defence of duress of circumstances to the charge of driving whilst disqualified.
- **The threat of death or serious injury must come from an external source**. Threats emanating from the defendant will not suffice. In *Rodger and Rose* [1998] 1 Cr App R 143 the defendants were not able to rely on duress of circumstances for charges arising from their escape from prison. They argued that prison was making them suicidal but it was held that internal threats would not suffice.
- **The defendant's conduct is only excused whilst the threat exists**. Continuation after the threat has expired will not be covered by the defence. In *DPP* v. *Bell* [1992] Crim LR 176 the defendant was able to rely on duress of circumstances to driving with excess alcohol as he only drove far enough to escape his attackers. In *DPP* v. *Jones* [1990] RTR 33, in similar circumstances, the defendant drove all the

way home and was not permitted to rely on the defence once the threat of death or serious harm had passed.

FURTHER READING

Clarkson, C.M.V., 'Necessary Action: a New Defence' [2004] *Criminal Law Review* 81. This article reviews the defences of duress (by threats and of circumstances) and argues that they could be amalgamated into a single defence of necessity. Looking at the theoretical justification for the existence of these defences, this article provides an excellent preparation for an essay on this topic.

Chapter summary:
Putting it all together

☐ Can you tick all the points from the revision checklist at the beginning of this chapter?

☐ Take the **end-of-chapter quiz** on the companion website.

☐ Test your knowledge of the cases with the **revision flashcards** on the website.

☐ Attempt the problem question from the beginning of the chapter using the guidelines below.

☐ Go to the companion website to try out other questions.

Answer guidelines

See the problem question at the start of the chapter. A diagram illustrating how to structure your answer is available on the website.

Points to remember when answering this question

■ Duress is a defence so establish liability for an offence before embarking on a discussion of duress.

■ Follow the instructions in the question. The focus is on property offences and Debbie's liability so there is no need to discuss the liability of Jenny or John, or Debbie's liability for common assault.

■ Untangle the facts and make a plan before starting to write your answer. There are three separate incidents that might give rise to liability so deal with each separately even though they all have a potential defence of duress.

■ The question makes reference to shoplifting. Remember that this is not a legal term and refer to it as theft; any discussion of Debbie's liability for shoplifting would lose marks.

■ Remember to use the facts to argue both for and against liability. For example, the potency of John's threat to Debbie will depend upon what she knows about him: whether he is prone to violence, whether he has beaten her in the past, any difference in their age or size.

Make your answer really stand out

■ Problems that require detailed focus on defences are often done badly. Many answers establish liability but give only cursory consideration to the defences. Make sure that you revise defences as thoroughly as offences and do not tackle a question that requires detailed knowledge of duress unless you can deal with it in sufficient depth.

■ Duress can cause difficulties because so much of its operation is open-ended; for example, the issue about membership of a gang is open to interpretation (Debbie is part of a 'group' which could be a gang and they are involved with unlawful activities but not necessarily violent ones; however they may have been known to commit robbery). Equally, if Debbie's brother has a reputation for violence, can this amount to voluntary association with a criminal as he is her brother (and presumably they live together)? Picking up on subtle nuances from the facts and incorporating them into your answer will gain credit from examiners.

■ Remember the need for immediacy in relation to the burglary. Debbie 'gives in eventually' which suggests that she was able to withstand the pressure for some time. Did she have any other options available to her? Where was her brother at the time of the burglary? Again, thoughtful use of the facts will make your answer stronger.

Conclusion

By using this revision guide to direct your work, you should now have a good knowledge and understanding of the way in which the various aspects of the criminal law work in isolation and the many ways in which they are interrelated. What is more, you should have acquired the necessary skills and techniques to demonstrate that knowledge and understanding in the exam, regardless of whether the questions are presented to you in essay or problem form.

TEST YOURSELF

- [ ] Look at the summary checklist of the points at the end of the book. Are you happy that you can now tick them all? If not, go back to the particular chapter and work through the material again. If you are still struggling, **seek help** from your tutor.

- [ ] Go to the companion website and revisit the interactive **quizzes** provided for each chapter.

- [ ] Make sure you can recall the **legal principles** of the key cases and statutory provisions which you have revised.

- [ ] Go to the companion website and test your knowledge of cases and terms with the **revision flashcards**.

Summary checklist

What you need to know:
- *Actus reus* and *mens rea* of all offences.
- Standard and burden of proof.
- Relationship between *actus reus* and *mens rea*.
- Problems surrounding need for coincidence of *actus reus* and *mens rea*.
- Nature of strict liability.
- Role and operation of defences.

CONCLUSION

- Types of *actus reus*.
- Role of *actus reus* in establishing criminal liability.
- Relationship between factual and legal causation.
- Circumstances when intervening acts will break the chain of causation.
- Situations giving rise to liability for failing to act.
- The types of *mens rea* and their role in establishing liability.
- The distinction between direct and oblique intention.
- The distinction between subjective and objective recklessness.
- The current tests on intention and recklessness to be applied in problem scenarios.
- The evolution of the current law on intention and recklessness.
- The operation of transferred malice.
- The *actus reus* and *mens rea* of the three inchoate offences.
- Why liability is imposed for inchoate offences.
- The relationship between conspiracy and incitement.
- The meaning of 'more than merely preparatory'.
- Distinction between joint principals and principal/accessories.
- Meaning of 'aid, abet, counsel and procure'.
- Intention and knowledge required by an accessory.
- Steps needed for effective withdrawal.
- Consequences of departure from a common plan.
- Role of causation and omissions.
- Distinction between implied and express malice.
- Scope of direct and oblique intention.
- Relationship between murder and manslaughter.
- Relationship between murder and voluntary manslaughter.
- Nature and operation of diminished responsibility.
- Two-stage test for provocation.
- Operation of the reasonable man test.
- Relationship between murder and involuntary manslaughter.
- Distinction between voluntary and involuntary manslaughter.
- Elements of constructive manslaughter.
- Operation of gross negligence manslaughter.
- Weaknesses in the law and proposals for reform.
- The relationship between OAPA, s.47 and common assault/battery.
- The meaning of 'bodily harm' (actual/grievous) and 'wounding'.
- The issues surrounding the *mens rea* of the offences: 'half *mens rea*' (s.47), *Mowatt* gloss (s.20), ulterior intent (s.18).
- Distinctions between SOA 2003 and the previous law.
- Role of consent, including operation of presumptions, in sexual offences.
- The relationship between the basic and aggravated offences.
- The scope of 'lawful excuse' and the role of 'consent' and 'protection of property'.
- The test of recklessness and implications of *R* v. *G*.
- Difficulties associated with the ownership, possession and transfer of property.

- Implications for theft of judicial interpretation of 'appropriation'.
- The *Ghosh* test of dishonesty.
- The 'thought rather than action' nature of intention permanently to deprive.
- The relationship between theft and burglary/robbery.
- The 'continuing act' approach to appropriation in robbery.
- Distinction between the two forms of burglary.
- Manifestations of deceptive behaviour.
- Relevance of timing of transfer of ownership.
- Operation of financial transactions.
- M'Naghten rules to establish insanity.
- Difference between medical and legal insanity.
- Relationship between insanity and automatism.
- Internal/external causes distinction.
- Distinction between voluntary and involuntary intoxication.
- Meaning of basic and specific intent and the relevance to intoxication.
- Clash of policy and principle in relation to intoxication.
- Relationship between self-defence and prevention of crime.
- Situations in which it is lawful to use force.
- Impact of mistaken belief on the necessity to use force.
- Determination of level of force that is appropriate.
- Operation of duress by threats and duress of circumstances.
- Availability of the defences and the rationale for their operation.
- Types of threat that suffice to establish duress.
- Circumstances that remove the defence of duress from the defendant.

Glossary of terms

Key definitions

Abetting	Implies consensus not causation
Aiding	Actual assistance, but neither consensus nor causation
Automatism	An act done by the muscles without any control by the mind
Battery	Any act by which a person intentionally or recklessly inflicts unlawful personal violence on another
Chain of causation	The link between the initial act of the defendant and the prohibited consequence
Common assault	An act by which a person intentionally or recklessly causes another to apprehend immediate and unlawful personal violence
Conduct crime	Those in which the *actus reus* is concerned with prohibited behaviour regardless of its consequences
Counselling	Implies consensus not causation
Deception	To induce a man to believe that a thing is true which is false and which the person practising the deceit knows or believes to be false
Direct intention	Corresponds with the everyday meaning of intention – aim, purpose or goal
Factual causation	Established using the 'but for' test: 'but for' the defendant's actions, the prohibited consequence would not have occurred
GBH	Really serious harm
Incitement	Encouraging or inducing another to commit an offence
Insanity	A defect of reason arising from a defect of mind such that the defendant did not know the nature and quality of his act or what he was doing was wrong
Intervening act	Something occurring after the defendant's act which breaks the chain of causation
Malice aforethought	Intention to kill or cause GBH

Murder	The unlawful killing of a reasonable person within the Queen's peace with malice aforethought
Procuring	Implies causation not consensus
Recklessness	A term used to describe culpable risk-taking
Result crime	Those in which the *actus reus* is defined in terms of prohibited consequences
Thin-skull rule	Requires that you 'take your victim as you find them' and are liable for harm caused to them even if they are particularly susceptible to that harm
Wound	A break in the continuity of both layers of the skin

Index